Born in Weston-super-Mare, John Cottrell entered journalism as a reporter with the *Bristol Evening Post* and later became a sports editor with Beaverbrook Newspapers. His "obsessive interest" in the Grand National dates back to 1961 when he first wrote about the race for *Sports Illustrated*, and subsequently his many articles on racing have been syndicated worldwide. Besides ghostwritten works, his sports books include *A Century of Great Soccer Drama* and *Man of Destiny*, a biography of Muhammad Ali.

The Punters' Guide to the Grand National

The Punters' Guide to the Grand National

John Cottrell

Published by SportsBooks Ltd

SportsBooks Limited
PO Box 422
Cheltenham
GL50 2YN
United Kingdom
Tel: 01242 256755
Fax: 01242 254694
e-mail info@sportsbooks.ltd.uk
Website www.sportsbooks.ltd.uk

A CIP catalogue record for this book is available from the British Library.

ISBN 9781899807 46 8
Printed by Creative Print and Design in Wales

Preface

THE GRAND NATIONAL is the greatest steeplechase on earth, unrivalled as a thrilling spectacle and a supreme test of raw courage, human and equine. It is also, in terms of gambling, the most magnetic of all sporting events, each year attracting more than £100 million in bets.

Such is its reputation for glorious unpredictability that it seems entirely appropriate that its first Aintree running – on Tuesday, February 26 1839 – should have been won by a nine-year-old bay gelding named *Lottery*, and originally called *Chance*.

But is that reputation deserved? In this book John Cottrell argues convincingly that, as the result of changed conditions, the Grand National is no longer a lottery; that, in reality, it offers the would-be punter excellent value.

"As will be shown", he writes, "the Grand National only remains such a perilous minefield because so many once-a-year punters bet without regard for well-proven guidelines."

He explains these simple guidelines and analyses in depth all the factors to be considered when seeking the Grand National winner. "By observing these guidelines," he writes, "the casual punter will not only avoid many pitfalls but greatly simplify the task of making selections by eliminating from the reckoning more than three-quarters of the runners."

Cottrell has written an original, easy-to-follow, step-by-step guide to betting on the Grand National. At the same time, in explaining his approach – evolved over decades of trial and error – he recaptures many of the most magical and dramatic moments in the National's illustrious history.

The idea, as he explains, is not to make a fortune. With stakes limited to £5 each-way, the winnings could never be sensational. But most valuably this multiple-betting approach netted such winners as ***Last Suspect*** (1985) at 50-1; ***Mr Frisk*** (1990), 16-1; ***Party Politics*** (1992), 14-1, ***Royal Athlete*** (1995), ***Red Marauder*** (2001), 33-1; and ***Monty's Pass*** (2003), 16-1. In addition there were often useful returns on placed horses.

Rather, the author's methods – as fully explained - are designed to achieve two aims: to show a profit for a modest outlay and, equally important, to give the punter every hope of enjoying sustained interest in watching the race - i.e. not having his or her involvement shattered with the fall of a single selection in the early stages.

Contents

INTRODUCTION

THE MAGIC AND THE MYTH

THE MAGIC of the Aintree Grand National may be readily defined by cognoscenti and laymen alike. It lies in its reputation for being an irresistible combination of glorious uncertainty and thrilling spectacle; and, above all, for being a supreme test of courage – human and equine – as up to forty challengers thunder around a pear-shaped course of four and a half miles that comprises 30 jumps followed by a stamina-sapping run-in of 494 yards to the finish.

It is quite simply the most famous steeplechase on earth, seen by an estimated 600 million television viewers in some 80 countries and each year attracting more than £100 million in bets; a race with 168 years of history that – more than any other sporting event – embraces an extraordinary wealth of drama and shocks, of heroic triumphs and heartbreaking failures.

Drama as enshrined in the story of the 1938 winner *Battleship*, a diminutive chestnut known as "the American pony", who – in the closest of all National finishes – triumphed by a head at 40-1, with 17-year-old Bruce Hobbs becoming the youngest-ever National winning jockey.

Shocks as exemplified by the 1928 winner *Tipperary Tim*, an ugly, ill-tempered 100-1 shot, who had a malformed "parrot mouth" and a metal tube in his throat to aid his breathing. Shortly before the "off", his amateur rider William Dutton was told, "Billy boy, you'll only win if all the others fall down"; and so it happened with 41 of 42 starters either falling or being pulled up.

Heroism as most famously displayed by the indomitable Bob Champion who, after a long battle against cancer and having been given only months to live, stormed back to win the 1981 National on *Aldaniti*, a chestnut gelding also making a comeback against all odds after three times breaking down with leg injuries.

Heart-breaking failure as experienced by Dick Francis in 1956 when the Queen Mother's *Devon Loch* inexplicably slithered into a pancake landing less than 50 yards from seemingly certain victory; and no less unfortunately evinced by the fate of 6ft 2in. tall Lord Mildmay of Flete who, in 1936, would surely have won on 100-1 outsider *Davy Jones* – if only his reins had not broken on landing over the penultimate fence.

The catalogue of extraordinary winners and losers is truly enormous, with Kipling's two imposters being most nobly represented by the unparalleled triple triumph of *Red Rum* and the cruel defeat of *Crisp*, the lion-hearted Australian chaser who, in 1973, was 15 lengths clear at the last only to be beaten three-quarters of a length when conceding 23lb. to the record-breaking *Rummy*.

THE MYTH of the Grand National, in contrast, is not so readily recognised. It is the popular belief that this is the most unpredictable race on earth and that it is entirely appropriate that its first well-documented running – on Tuesday, February 26 1839 – should have been won by a nine-year-old bay gelding named *Lottery*, and originally called *Chance.*

This generally held view was well summarised on the eve of the 1995 National by an article in the London *Evening Standard* which stated: "The real racegoers rather despise the whole affair. The field is too big, the course too hazardous for the expert to predict the result with any confidence. It's a race for the mug punters and the housewives".

Ostensibly, this myth is well supported by events. For example, on April 8 1995, British bookmakers celebrated one of the most profitable Grand Nationals ever. An estimated £30 million had been gambled on a race in which the market leaders finished nowhere and the four placed horses were priced at 40-1, 16-1, 100-1 and 9-1 respectively. A spokesman for William Hill described it as "a dream result".

But the reality is very different. The fact is that if most punters had followed well-proven guidelines – as I shall later explain – the 1995 Grand National would have been "a nightmare result" for the layers. Indeed, on the evidence of our experience over the past two decades, the National is one of the most inviting races for the ordinary punter aiming to make a modest profit.

Following that "shock" victory of *Royal Athlete* in 1995, *The Times* carried an article under the joint byline of Julian Muscat and Richard Evans. Those esteemed racing experts wrote about "the unpredictability of the result, with a 40-1 winner, followed home by horses priced at 16-1 and 100-1".

They went on: "The unlikely success of *Royal Athlete*, the comeback by another 'old crock', *Party Politics*, in second place, and the run of a lifetime by the amateur-ridden *Over The Deel* have revived the romance of the world's most famous steeplechase. It is a race where glorious uncertainty prevails."

Thus, on the strength of such hyperbole, the great myth about the Grand National lives on.

But wait. If the Grand National is really so unpredictable, how come that the aforementioned Julian Muscat tipped the "unlikely" 1995 winner on the morning of the race, while Gerald Hubbard, *The Times'* Private Handicapper, selected four from the field – 1. *Master Oats*, 2. *Party Politics*, 3. *Royal Athlete*, 4. *Dubacilla* – that brilliantly included three of the four horses in the frame?

The following year, incidentally, Hubbard did even better. In making his selections – 1. *Rough Quest*, 2. *Encore Un Peu*, 3, *Bishops Hall*, 4. *Young Hustler* – he achieved the hugely rewarding Straight Forecast (first and second in correct order) while his fourth horse finished fifth! Moreover, former champion jockey Peter Scudamore also selected *Rough Quest* and *Encore Un Peu* to finish first and second.

So far I have been referring to the chances of finding the winner from a maximum of 40 runners. If, as popularly maintained, this is so difficult to achieve, then surely it must be nigh impossible to pick the winner from the original entry of more than 100 horses. But no. In February 1998, when 105 entries were declared, the *Racing Post's Pricewise* (then Melvyn Collier) advised punters to take the 25-1 on offer for *Earth Summit*. His selection won at 7-1.

A once-in-a-lifetime fluke? By no means. In 2003 the National was reputedly the most competitive of all time with so much quality that 33 of the 40 starters were in the handicap proper. Yet *Pricewise* (now Tom Segal) picked out *Monty's Pass* from a record entry of 149. His selection, 40-1 at that stage, won at 16-1.

Again, in 2006, when 148 entries were declared, both *Pricewise* and Rob Wright, *The Times,* picked out *Numbersixvalverde* as the one to back at 25-1. He won at 11-1.

No less remarkable were the predictions for the 2000 Grand National. On the morning of the race *Pricewise* (Melvyn Collier) made his recommendation under the headline: "*Papillon* at 33-1 Makes Sense". His tip was also the selection of the *Racing Post's* Mel Cullinan and Tom Segal, and of their Irish correspondent Tony O'Hehir. Moreover, *Papillon* was the most favoured choice when racing correspondents were polled in an eve-of-the-National BBC TV preview. The result was an estimated £10 million payout to punters with *Papillon* winning at 10-1. Some lottery!

This is not to suggest that following tipsters is a sure path for punters seeking success in the National. On the contrary, as later shown (see Chapter 23, Tipsters), their spectacular successes have been well matched by the most dismal failures. Nonetheless, based on my own experience, I conclude that the Grand National is far from being the most unpredictable of races.

Yet I know of only one racing correspondent who has strongly supported my view. In 1990 Jon Freeman wrote in the *Sunday Times*: "Contrary to popular belief the Grand National is not racing's ultimate lottery. You get the odd daft result, particularly when the ground is soft, but no more than in any other race, and as a rule the finish is fought out by horses whose form entitles them to be there."

How true. Moreover, most advantageously, no other steeplechase is preceded by such a wealth of information and in-depth analysis of the runners, so enabling the industrious punter – by following principles recommended here – to narrow down the field to just a handful of possible winners.

In his book, *World Of Betting*, racing pundit John McCririck rightly says: "Put not your faith in systems. If there were even one that consistently worked, whether at the track or in the casino, everyone would have cottoned on to it by now." However, he does recognise that a number of systems are more logical than others. And this even applies to the so-called "lottery" of the Grand National.

As this work explains in detail there is just one betting system, more logical than others, that does have a considerable degree of proven merit when applied to the Grand National. This is the Elimination Method that involves eliminating all those horses which, based on statistical evidence and other key factors, are unlikely to have any chance of success.

Here I will examine and assess those factors in depth to show how a field of up to 40 runners may be reduced to a workable number – not more than six – for betting purposes. And while recognising that no system is infallible, I will show how this approach, faithfully followed, resulted in backing such long-shot winners as *Last Suspect* (50-1) and *Royal Athlete* (40-1) and even found the 33-1 winner (*Red Marauder*) of the 2001 National which saw only four horses finish in quagmire conditions.

Chapter 1

ANTE-POST BETTING

THE FASCINATING "Find the Grand National winner" puzzle begins every year in February when, almost two months before the running of the race, the senior handicapper announces the weights he has allotted to more than a hundred entries. Here the would-be punter is subject to enormous temptation: the chance to back one or more horses at ante-post odds far more inviting than those likely to be available on the day of the race. Punter, BEWARE!

This is a temptation to be strongly resisted. The chances of a horse being withdrawn in the next two months are high; and, whatever the reason for an entry failing to make the line-up, the stake on a non-runner is lost unless the bookmaker has made a special "with a run" declaration. Moreover, ante-post favourites have an appalling record. Since 1990, on publication of the weights, there have been 27 clear favourites or joint market leaders. Fourteen of these were subsequently withdrawn or failed to make the cut; and of the remainder only six completed the course. Just four finished in the frame – *Suny Bay*, second (1998); *Moorcroft Boy*, third (1994); *Papillon*, fourth (2001); and *Clan Royal*, third (2006). None was a winner.

Not atypical was the experience of ante-post punters in 1999. That year, *Double Thriller* and *Teeton Mill* were the early favourites. The latter was subsequently withdrawn. The former became all the rage, for a time as short as 4-1, the tightest odds since *Poethlyn* won at 11-4 in 1919. But he drifted on the day to 7-1 and then fell at the first fence. Also heavily backed ante-post was the Martin Pipe-trained seven-year-old *Eudipe*, cut from 20-1 to 10-1. He fell fatally at the second Becher's.

The history of the race is littered with such examples of huge losses being incurred by ante-post punters who never had a real run for their money. An especially sad case was in 2001 when the *Racing Post's* highly influential *Pricewise* highlighted the prospects of *Cavalero*, a 66-1 chance. Punters responded but shortly afterwards the 12-year-old had to be put down after breaking his back in a fall at Warwick.

In 2002, when the weights were announced, *Moor Lane* was a strongly tipped, well-backed 14-1 market leader – absurdly so since he needed 31 defectors to get a run. He missed the cut by two places. In 2003, yet another, albeit rare, circumstance thwarted many ante-post punters. *Davids Lad*, joint favourite, was banned for 42 days under the non-triers' rule, keeping him off the racecourse until two days after the showpiece at Aintree. One punter had staked £25,000 on the horse and was left sweating for weeks on a series of appeals that went as far as the Supreme Court in Dublin. All the appeals were dismissed.

In 2004, ante-post "thieves" were hit hard when *Timbera*, as short as 8-1 favourite, was a late withdrawal due to a lung infection. Similarly, many were losers in 2005 when a slight leg injury put out *Silver Birch*, impressive winner of the Welsh National. And again *Timbera* was costly, being the ante-post choice of *Pricewise* at 33-1, only to be retired after breaking down on his seasonal reappearance.

Nevertheless, despite this dismal record, the temptation to bet ante-post remains compelling – most especially in the light of the few brilliant tips that have occurred at the time of publication of the weights – i.e. the aforementioned recommendations of *Pricewise* to back *Earth Summit* at 25-1, *Monty's Pass* at 40-1 and *Numbersixvalverde* at 25-1.

If you are still irresistibly inclined to place an ante-post bet, I advise limiting it to a harmless outlay and so not risking ruining the big day before it has even begun. Thus, when the weights were revealed in 2005, I simply had £2 win bets at 25-1 on two strongly fancied horses: *Timbera* and *Hedgehunter*. £2 was lost when the former was withdrawn. On the other hand, there was a £50 gain when the latter won as 7-1 favourite.

But such tiny ante-post outlays are strictly speculative "fun bets", not any part of the recommended Elimination Method. Meanwhile, even at this stage – two months before the National – the elimination process can be initiated.

Subsequent sections now assess, in alphabetical order, those factors which punters may consider in making their selections; and they address the reasons for and against eliminating horses on specific grounds.

Chapter 2

AGE

DURING THE two months prior to the Grand National, more than one hundred entries will be reduced to a maximum of forty. In advance, there is no way of telling which ones will be withdrawn because of injury, sickness, loss of form or the prospect of facing unsuitable ground conditions. Nor is it certain that horses way out of the handicap will be eliminated. Remarkably, in 1998, there were 105 entries and, as it happened, not one was too low in the weights to make the 40-runner cut. There were so many withdrawals that three horses allotted the bottom weight of 7st. 10lb. qualified to run off the minimum 10st.

Nevertheless, despite so many imponderables, I was already prepared at the initial entry stage to make my own eliminations – solely on the grounds of age.

For more than half a century I have automatically dismissed all horses not in the eight-to-twelve age range, and so far, touch wood, I have never lived to regret it.

Statistically, the case for such action is obvious. Since seven-year-old *Bogskar* triumphed in 1940 all winners have been at least eight years old. And since 13-year-old *Sergeant Murphy* scored in 1923, all winners have been no more than twelve. But it is more than just statistics that persuades me to eliminate horses under eight and over twelve.

First, consider six-year-olds. During the 19th century they won thirteen Grand Nationals, including four in succession (1882–85). Since then only two have scored – the last, *Ally Soper* in 1915. Of course, that decline may be partly explained by the fact that, in modern times, very few of this age have appeared. Indeed, for twelve years (1987 until 1998) the race was restricted to horses seven years and upwards.

However, since they were readmitted in 1999, six-year-olds have not made any impression. Eight have since run in the National. Of these, two fell at the first fence and only two got beyond the sixth, Becher's. The most successful were *Majed*, who fell at the 22nd in 2002, and the Paul Nicholls-trained *L'Aventure*, who finished 15th in 2005 – the first time in 65 years that a six-year-old had even completed the course.

Trainer Martin Pipe led the way with six-year-old entries, his *Tamarindo* (1999) falling at the first Becher's and his *Royal Predica* (2000) going out at the first. That latter year he had also entered the brilliant *Gloria Victis*, whose enormous potential was reflected in his allotted weight, 11st. 10lb. But tragically this most impressive winner of the *Racing Post* Chase perished in the Cheltenham Gold Cup, falling fatally two out when in strong contention.

It was the most distressing experience of champion jockey Tony McCoy's career, and he was angered by so many letters arguing that it was not right to run a six-year-old novice of such great potential in the most demanding of championship steeplechases. He said, "To me it didn't matter if he was a five-year-old or ten-year-old, he was that good". Maybe. But serious doubts must remain as to whether six-year-olds are strong enough for the marathon test of the Grand National.

The case against seven-year-olds is not quite so

compelling. They are known to have won at least 22 Grand Nationals, including three in succession in the 1930s. (The age of a few early winners is unknown since horses seven years and over were then sometimes simply listed as "Aged".) But most of these successes were in the 19th century. Since *Bogskar* won the only wartime National, seven-year-olds have finished second on six occasions; more significantly, one has not even been placed since 1971 when *Black Secret* went down by a neck to *Specify*.

Why have they faded into relative obscurity? One simple answer is that they have been handicapped numerically. In 1947, as many as 10 seven-year-olds ran in the National. In the whole of the 1960s, however, only 18 of 360 starters were seven-years-olds. In the 1970s, 15 of 364 runners were aged seven. Then, in the 1980s, came an all-time low with just four seven-year-olds among 398 starters. Only seven appeared in the 1990s, eleven so far in this century.

The decline in numbers could be explained by the fact that, in the light of more advanced training methods, many trainers had come to recognize that seven-year-olds are not quite mature enough for such a vigorous test as the National. Thus quantity eventually gave way to quality. Between 1980 and 1999, six of the 11 seven-year-olds completed the course, whereas in the 1960s and 1970s, the overwhelming majority had failed to finish. On the other hand, since 1999 only one of twelve (*Majed*, 12th in 2003) has managed to finish.

Even seven-year-olds of the highest quality have failed to be placed in the National. In 1977 *Davy Lad* was a 10-1 shot after winning the Cheltenham Gold Cup by six lengths. He fell at Aintree's first open ditch, broke down the following season and was forced to retire as an eight-year-old. In 1994 *Young Hustler* went to Aintree after finishing a creditable third in the Gold Cup. There he was unluckily brought down at the 11th.

On one occasion, in 1989, the supreme lady trainer Jenny Pitman ventured to run a seven-year-old (*Team Challenge*) in the National. He had taken third place at Cheltenham in the three-mile Kim Muir Memorial Handicap Chase. Now, at Aintree, he was going so well that, four out, jockey Michael Bowlby thought he might win. But the seven-year-old tired and finished ninth. "He did not really see it out", said Bowlby. "He will be better next year".

It was a familiar story. In the 1963 National, seven-year-old *Carrickbeg* had been runner-up, beaten only three-quarters of a length by *Ayala*. It is noteworthy that his amateur rider, John Lawrence (now Lord Oaksey) later told me that *Carrickbeg* markedly improved from the ages of seven to eight and that he might well have been good enough to win the 1964 National if he had not been put out by an injury when winning at Sandown the previous January.

Interestingly, seven-year-olds have an outstanding record in the Irish Grand National. But that fiercely competitive, often gruelling, chase at Fairyhouse is run over three-and-a-half miles. The extra mile at Aintree can make all the difference in testing a horse's strength and stamina; and the record suggests that a horse is best suited to such a marathon challenge after reaching full maturity at the age of eight or nine.

In recent years a few trainers (primarily the now retired Martin Pipe) have continued to enter seven-year-olds. But invariably they have disappointed: in 1997, *Evangelica*, the last of 17 finishers; 1998, *Damas*, refused 11th, and *Decyborg*, pulled up 27th; 1999, *Eudipe*, fell fatally at the second Becher's, and *Castle Coin*, knocked over 25th; 2000, *Village King*, fell 20th; 2001, *Spanish Main*, fell 1st, and *Tresor de Mai*, fell 2nd; 2003, *Iris Bleu*, pulled up 16th, and *Majed*, finished a distant 12th at 200-1. And two of those seven-year-olds – *Eudipe* and *Iris Bleu* – were well-fancied contenders, having the assistance of the most successful jump jockey of all time, A.P. McCoy.

Above all, McCoy believed he had a great chance of scoring his elusive first National win on the French-bred *Jurancon II*, one of four co-favourites in the 2004 race. *Jurancon II* had an excellent record; indeed, the handicapper said he would have given him an extra stone if framing the weights after his most recent win. Yet the so well-backed youngster fell at the fourth. Other seven-year-olds in the race were: *Shardam*, unseated rider at the third; *Montreal*, fell at the sixth; and *Royal Atalza*, a 100-1 shot, never dangerous though he did get as far as the 28th before being pulled up. In 2005, the only seven-year-old in the field, *Double Honour*, was disputing second place when he unseated his rider at the 21st. In 2006 two made it to the line-up. *Whispered Secret* unseated his rider at the first, *Le Duc* at the eighth (Canal Turn).

Quite possibly, more six and seven-year-olds will appear in future because the number of French imports has increased hugely in recent years. In France, jump racing has always been distinctly different in that horses there are schooled over fences at a very early age, often as two-year-olds in November and December; and then, as three-year-olds, they may begin hurdling in March and perhaps chasing in September. In contrast, their

British and Irish counterparts tend not to be schooled until they are four or five, and they usually only develop into mature chasers at the age of seven or eight.

British buyers have become more adept at spotting young French horses that have had few races and are less liable to an early burn-out. Nonetheless, in recent years the only French-bred horses to run with distinction in the National have been *Encore un Peu*, *Mely Moss* and *Clan Royal*, all runners-up at the age of nine, and *Royal Auclair*, finishing second as an eight-year-old. There has not been a French-bred winner since *Lutteur 111* in 1909.

In recent years so many precocious French horses have been imported that it may well be that a seven-year-old winner of the National will eventually emerge. But until it happens, we will continue to eliminate challengers of that age.

At the other end of the scale, history is even more strongly against horses more than twelve years old. Only two 13-year-olds are recorded as National winners: *Why Not* (1894) and *Sergeant Murphy* (1923). Since the latter success, only three have even been placed: *Overshadow* (third, 1953), *Eternal* (fourth, 1964) and *Rondetto* (third, 1969). There has never been a 14-year-old winner and *Schubert* (1948) and *Cylduffe* (1949) were the last of that age to complete the course, finishing 13th and 10th respectively.

With such a dismal record, it is surprising that so many 13-year-olds are still entered. In 1999 three made it to the Aintree line-up: *Mudahim*, a past winner of the Irish National, unseated his rider at the first Becher's; *Commercial Artist*, pulled up at the 17th; and *Camelot Knight*, fell at the 22nd. In 2001 the field included no fewer than four 13-year-olds: *Brave Highlander*, fell 19th; *Feels Like Gold*, fell 8th; *Merry People*, unseated rider, 7th; and *Addington Boy*, brought down, 2nd. In 2005, as the defending champion, *Amberleigh House* was a well-supported 13-year-old, but he finished a never challenging tenth and, returning the following year, he was pulled up before the 21st. That same year the three 13-year-olds – *First Gold*, *Rince Ri* and *Native Upmanship* – were 100-1 shots that failed to get round. Remarkably, the best result by a 13-year-old since 1969 was achieved in 1994 when 51-year-old Mrs Rosemary Henderson rode her 100-1 outsider, *Fiddlers Pike*, into fifth place.

Which age group has the best record in the National? A nine-year-old (*Lottery*) triumphed in the first-ever National of 1839 and this group has been predominant ever since. It has provided at least 43 winners, and 33 of these in the 20th century – including a hat-trick (1910–12) and four successive Nationals (1948–51). Unusually, there was an eight-year gap (1989–96) without a nine-year-old winner. But then came the victory of *Lord Gyllene* in 1997. Two years later nine-year-olds – *Bobbyjo*, *Blue Charm* and *Call It A Day* – filled the first three places; and in 2000 the age group again had the winner and runner-up with *Papillon* and *Mely Moss* respectively. *Hedgehunter* was another nine-year-old winner in 2005.

Since the easing of fences (notably Becher's) in 1990, eleven-year-olds have matched the nine-year-olds in scoring four wins; also the group has had the fastest winner of them all, *Mr Frisk*. Next, in this period, come ten-year-olds with four wins, followed by eight and 12-year-olds with two wins apiece. Most unusually, in

1992, eight-year-olds filled the first three places with *Party Politics*, *Romany King* and *Laura's Beau*; and ten years later they provided the winner (*Bindaree*) and the runner-up (*What's Up Boys*).

Conclusion: *Eliminate any six or seven-year-old in the Grand National field, plus any over the age of twelve.*

Chapter 3

AMATEUR RIDERS

IT WAS in 1963, as a novice punter, that I first tinkered with the elimination approach to seeking a Grand National winner. It was a complete failure – the idea having been naively conceived on reading an article by the great Peter O'Sullevan in the *Daily Express*.

On the morning of the 1963 National O'Sullevan analysed all the 47 runners. In the process he pointed out that it was 40 years since a 13-year-old had won; that no horse handicapped at 10st. 10lb. had won since *Emblem* in 1863; that only three mares had won in the past 60 years; that only five horses in National history had won the race twice; that there had been no owner-trained winner since *Bogskar* in 1940; that not for 79 years had a horse sired by a Derby winner succeeded; and that no amateur rider had even ridden into a place since "Phonsie" O'Brien was on the 1957 runner-up *Royal Tan* in 1957.

Simplistically, on this basis, I eliminated fourteen runners at a stroke. But that still left 33 contenders and I was no nearer to finding the shock winner, *Ayala* at 66-1. Clearly, at the time, with 21 horses running from out of the handicap and 29 priced at 50-1 or more, an elimination system had no merit – a fact conclusively confirmed by *Foinavon's* absurd 100-1 victory in 1967. Only from the 1980s onwards, after costly trial and error, was I encouraged to pursue that approach.

The 1963 experiment did at least provide one useful lesson: that it was ridiculous to eliminate a horse because it had an amateur rider. Of the fourteen I had eliminated, only one finished in a place: *Carrickbeg*, beaten by just three-quarters of a length after looking all over the winner 50 yards out. He was ridden by the remarkably versatile John Lawrence, a journalist who, within minutes of finishing exhausted in the National, was dashing off to file a moving and detailed 1,000-word report for the *Sunday Telegraph*.

As history shows, the Grand National is one of the few major sporting events in which amateurs can take on professionals with a degree of success. They have done so successfully on 40 occasions.

To be sure, only five amateurs have ridden the winner since the 1946 resumption of the race after World War II; and only one (Marcus Armytage on *Mr Frisk*, 1990) in the past 24 years. However, there have also been five post-war instances of an amateur riding into second place. Most notably those include John Lawrence (now Lord Oaksey); Jim Dreaper shaded by only a neck on *Black Secret* (1971); and Colin Magnier, just three-quarters of a length second on *Greasepaint* (1983).

It is noteworthy that the fastest and third fastest Grand National winning times have been achieved by amateur-ridden horses: *Mr Frisk* (1990) and *Grittar* (1982), ridden by Dick Saunders. More recently an amateur (Chris Bonner) has twice finished in a place: third in 1995 on *Over The Deel* at 100-1 and the following year with 33-1 chance *Sir Peter Lely*, only a short head behind third-placed *Superior Finish*.

Conclusion: *Never eliminate horses simply because they are to be amateur-ridden.*

Chapter 4

BLINKERS

IT HAS been suggested that blinkered horses are at a disadvantage in the Grand National because they are less able to see the threat of interference when caught in heavy traffic. However, in 2001, a Liverpool University study to identify risk factors for falling concluded that blinkers had no obvious influence either way in races over fences.

Nevertheless, in modern times only four National winners have run in blinkers – *Battleship* (1938), *Foinavon* (1967), *L'Escargot* (1975) and *Earth Summit* (1998). Counter balancing this discouraging statistic is the fact that only a minority of horses – roughly one in ten – have gone to the post with headgear, either blinkers or visor (blinkers with slits for limited viewing).

The fact remains that since *L'Escargot's* success, more than 130 runners have worn blinkers with only one managing to win. In 2001, when only the first two of four finishers had not been remounted, the runner-up *Smarty* was equipped with blinkers. Again, in 2002, a blinkered runner, *What's Up Boys*, ran a blinder to finish a close second to *Bindaree.*

Earth Summit is a classic example of a horse which hugely improved when fitted with blinkers. Similarly, *What's Up Boys* was helped to concentrate by the blinkers he had first worn when finishing fifth in the 2002 Cheltenham Gold Cup. But these are more the exception than the rule. Moreover, it does not automatically follow that a horse who has run well with first-time blinkers will be suited by them a second time.

This warning was sounded by Tony McCoy before riding *Dark Stranger* in the 2000 National. He said, "Often horses shine in blinkers on their debut and then disappoint if they get used to their effect." And so it was with *Dark Stranger*. The 9-1 favourite fell at the third in the 2000 National.

More certainly, there is a mass of evidence to support the belief that blinkered horses, when running without a rider to guide them, are much more likely to cause mayhem because they are unable to see rivals about to wander across their line of vision. Most infamously it was a riderless, blinkered horse, *Popham Down*, that caused the huge pile-up in 1967, bringing almost the entire field to a standstill. Similarly, in 2001, the blinkered *Paddy's Return* veered sharply across the Canal Turn, putting out ten horses in the process. That year he was one of no fewer than ten runners wearing either blinkers or a visor.

As observed by three times champion jockey Stan Mellor, the wearing of blinkers resulted in loose horses behaving unnaturally and running across the pack. And subsequently there was some support for his view that the wearing of blinkers in the National should be banned.

The situation was reviewed by the Aintree management, the Jockey Club and the National Trainers' Federation. The six regional bodies of the NTF were unanimous that horses needing blinkers still be allowed to wear them, and their view was accepted.

But should a horse be eliminated by the punter simply because he or she is equipped with headgear?

In 2001 a Jockey Club study concluded that horses with headgear have a worse record in the National than those without; at that time, in the 26 years since *L'Escargot's* success, there had been only one winner out of 105 horses going to post equipped with headgear. But, in the light of two relatively recent runners-up having headgear, this is not a compelling argument for automatically dismissing blinkered runners.

Conclusion: *A horse should only be eliminated on blinker-wearing grounds if, after following the first two stages of the elimination process (see Chapter 26), it is necessary to reduce the field still further to achieve a workable remainder (not more than six) for betting purposes.*

Chapter 5

BREEDING

WHEN IT comes to National Hunt racing, breeding is by no means a sure guide to a horse's prospects. *Red Rum*, for example, sired by a champion miler out of a rogue-mare, was certainly not an obvious candidate for greatness over fences. Moreover, the Grand National Hall of Fame is packed with winners that were cheaply bred (*Teal*, most remarkably, was once on offer at £2. 10s.) and they come in all shapes and sizes – ranging from the gigantic (over 17 hands) and ungainly *Moifaa* to the diminutive (15 hands 2in.) dual winners *Abd-El-Kader* and *The Lamb*.

On the other hand, it has occasionally been profitable to follow certain bloodlines. Outstanding examples: *My Prince*, sire of winners of four Grand Nationals, plus great jumpers who were placed in five others; *Ascetic*, *Cottage* and *Vulcan*, all of whom sired three winners; and – most prominent in modern times – *Roselier* who has been responsible for 18 Grand National runners, among them winners *Royal Athlete* and *Bindaree*, dual runner-up *Suny Bay*, *Moorcroft Boy* (third), *Ebony Jane* and *Kingsmark* (fourth), and seven more who completed the course.

Two more of note are *Menelek*, sire of National winners *Hallo Dandy* and *Rag Trade*, and *Crash Course*, sire of winner *Rough Quest*, plus runner-up *Romany King* and *Esha Ness*, first home in the 1993 void National.

Conclusion: *Breeding may be a factor of interest for the aficionado but I do not regard it as sufficiently useful to include in the elimination process.*

Chapter 6

CHELTENHAM FESTIVAL FORM

THE WEIGHTS for the Grand National are framed before the staging of the Cheltenham Festival. Therefore, the senior handicapper is unable to take into consideration outstanding performances at National Hunt's greatest meeting. But how far does Cheltenham Festival form provide a useful guide to prospects in the National? And, most pertinently, does the National come too soon after the supreme championship of steeplechasing: the Cheltenham Gold Cup, a gruelling test over three miles two and a half furlongs, with a stamina-sapping 237-yard uphill finish?

The two most celebrated chases are usually only about three weeks apart, and occasionally, because of the moveable feast of Easter, as few as fifteen days apart. The difficulty of performing well in both races is fairly reflected in the fact that only one horse, *Golden Miller* (1934), has ever achieved the Gold Cup–National double.

The first of many to try and fail was *Conjuror II* who, after being a head second in the inaugural Gold Cup of 1924, became the 5-2 favourite for the National, the shortest priced starter since *Regal* in 1879. It seemed perfectly logical since *Conjuror II* had been an unlucky third in the 1923 National and he was still on 11st. for Aintree despite his great run under 12st. at Cheltenham.

His failure in the National could be excused since he was an unlucky faller – being baulked when going well by a riderless horse at Becher's Brook.

Nevertheless, an ominous pattern was soon to emerge. *Ballinode* (1925), *Koko* (1926) and *Thrown In* (1927) were all well-backed fallers at Aintree following victory in the Gold Cup.

In 1929 *Easter Hero* restored some faith in Cheltenham form when, after a 20-length Gold Cup success, he courageously carried a top weight of 12st. 7lb. in the National to finish six lengths second in a record field of 66 runners. On the other hand, a compelling argument against running a horse in both events was provided by the experience of *Grakle*. Six times between 1927 and 1932 the bay gelding ran in the National. Significantly, his victory came in the one year (1931) when, due to abandonment because of frost, he was not made to go to Cheltenham before Aintree.

In 1934 the negative "Cheltenham factor" was magnificently overcome as the great *Golden Miller* triumphed in the National just 16 days after achieving his third successive Gold Cup. But this was one horse in a million. The following year, when *Thomond II* again finished third in the National, it was widely considered that he would have won but for the fact that, fifteen days earlier, he had had a desperately hard race in the Gold Cup, going down by only three-quarters of a length after a titanic duel with the *Miller*.

That year, and again in 1936 after his fifth successive Gold Cup victory, *Golden Miller* failed to finish in the National under a massive 12st. 7lb. It now became rare for a horse to appear in both of the great chases – the best efforts in the next two decades being put up by

Prince Regent, winner of the 1946 Gold Cup and then third as 3-1 favourite in the National, and by *Mont Tremblant*, unplaced in the 1953 Gold Cup and then 20-lengths second in the National.

In 1973, however, there came an extraordinary triple challenge by Gold Cup runners. At Cheltenham, *L'Escargot*, *Crisp* and *Spanish Steps* had finished fourth, fifth and sixth respectively. At Aintree, 16 days later, they finished third, second and fourth respectively. Only *Red Rum*, winning with a 23lb. advantage in record time, spoiled their challenge.

Subsequently, it was noteworthy that *L'Escargot*, the 1970 and 1971 Gold Cup winner, did best at Aintree when he had not previously raced at Cheltenham – being runner-up to *Red Rum* in 1974 and winning from *Red Rum* as a 12-year-old in 1975. And then came two events that strongly discouraged running a Gold Cup winner in the following Grand National.

In 1977, *Davy Lad* won the Gold Cup by six lengths and looked well in for Aintree on only 10st. 13lb. But he was only seven years old and in the National he fell at the first open ditch and was retired the following season after breaking down. Two years later *Alverton* went to Aintree sixteen days after winning the Gold Cup by a devastating 25 lengths. Now, on 10st. 13lb. instead of 12st., he also appeared to be a handicap snip; and he was looking unbeatable as he cruised on to the second circuit. But, astonishingly, he crashed into the Becher's fence and broke his neck on hitting the ground – such a strange error that it was speculated that he had suffered a heart attack before the fall that ended hopes of emulating *Golden Miller's* double.

It was not until the 1990s, following modifications

to Aintree's fences, that owners and trainers became more prepared to see a horse tackle the Gold Cup and National in the same season. And, in 1991, it seemed almost certain that *Golden Miller's* unique double would at last be equalled. Just 23 days after his short-head victory at Cheltenham, *Garrison Savannah* was lightly handicapped on 11st. 1lb., jumping superbly well, and leading by eight lengths when over the last. But cruelly the slogging run-in found him out. He began to falter at The Elbow and just one hundred yards out *Seagram* swept past to win by five lengths.

The following year *Cool Ground* carried the same weight at Aintree, also 23 days after a short-head win in the Gold Cup. He trailed in tenth. Next, in 1994, Gold Cup winner *The Fellow* was backed down to 9-1 at Aintree. But the heavy ground was hopelessly against him and he crashed out from sheer exhaustion at the Canal Turn second time around.

In 1995 *Master Oats* became the eleventh horse attempting to match *Golden Miller's* double. Having won the Gold Cup by an impressive 15 lengths, he went off in the National as the hot 5-1 favourite. But without his favoured soft ground he was outpaced and dropped away over the last half-mile to finish seventh. Interestingly, the 40-1 winner *Royal Athlete* had been third in the 1993 Gold Cup before one month later falling at the tenth in the void National. In 1995, when triumphant as a 12-year-old at Aintree, he had been a late withdrawal from the Cheltenham test.

Thus, history remains strongly against any Gold Cup winner appearing in the National of the same year. On the other hand, there is some encouragement for backing National contenders who have been beaten in the Gold Cup. In 1994, *Miinnehoma*, a poor seventh at Cheltenham, won at Aintree. Most notably, in 1996, the Gold Cup runner-up went on to win the National, albeit in a year when only 27 horses lined up for the starter.

That year, in a signed statement featured in full-page Coral advertisements, great jockey John Francome declared: "Even in what looks a substandard National, one horse I cannot see winning is the Cheltenham Gold Cup runner-up *Rough Quest*. He has had a hard race and has had only two weeks to recover from it." But *Rough Quest*, due to run off a 19lb. higher mark, was an extraordinary handicap snip on 10st. 7lb. Going off as the 7-1 favourite, he became the first horse since 1934 to win at Aintree after being placed in the Gold Cup.

His so favourable weight was the critical factor; also there was such a relatively small field. Not so fortunate was the grey *Suny Bay* who, in 1998, just sixteen days after being fifth in the Gold Cup, put in a stupendous run at Aintree to finish runner-up for the second year in succession. He was conceding 23lb. to the winner *Earth Summit*. Similarly, in 2002, another grey, *What's Up Boys*, was also a brilliant National runner-up after being fifth in the Gold Cup. Again, he was on a big weight, giving almost a stone to *Bindaree* who won by just one length and three-quarters. But arguably the most glorious failure of all those seeking both Gold Cup and National success was *Hedgehunter* in 2006. After racing superbly to be runner-up at Cheltenham he went to Aintree on the top weight of 11st. 12lb. There, with overnight rain crucially counting against him, he went down by six lengths to *Numbersixvalverde* who enjoyed an 18lb. advantage.

As for Cheltenham form in general – excluding the Gold Cup – overall, horses placed in Festival races have a bad record in the National of the same year. In 1991 *Seagram* won the Ritz Club before going on to victory at Aintree. But he remains the only Festival winner to have prevailed in the following National since 1961 when *Nicolaus Silver* scored seventeen days after his success in the Kim Muir Memorial Challenge Cup. Indeed, in the last ten years only one horse has even run at Cheltenham before winning at Aintree: *Bindaree* (2002), who had finished seventh in the William Hill Handicap Chase. That year, unusually, both the second and third had also run at the Festival.

However, looking back at Festival form in earlier seasons, it is worth noting Grand National contenders who had run in Cheltenham's Royal Sun Alliance in their novice year. This has thrown up a remarkable number of National winners – among them *Corbiere*, *West Tip*, *Rhyme 'N' Reason*, *Mr Frisk*, *Miinnehoma*, *Royal Athlete* and *Rough Quest* – plus Jenny Pitman's unlucky non-winners *Esha Ness* and *Garrison Savannah*.

Conclusion: *Excepting a runner that – like Rough Quest – has an extraordinarily favourable weight, there is a case for eliminating any horse that goes to Aintree after having had a particularly hard race at Cheltenham. This is to be put into operation if too many runners remain after completing Stage One of the elimination process.*

Chapter 7

DISTANCE

THE GRAND NATIONAL is the longest race run in Britain under Jockey Club Rules – a marathon test of jumping and stamina covering four miles and 856 yards. Which horses are most likely to excel over such a distance?

It might seem obvious for a punter to look for a horse that has already proven ability to get the trip. Yet, after the 1970 success of *Gay Trip*, who had previously never won over as far as three miles, there developed a popular theory – strongly supported by the most successful Grand National trainer Fred Rimell – that a two-and-a-half-miler with a touch of class was ideally suited to the race.

This notion gained added support from the victory of *Specify* in 1971 and two years later from the stupendous run of *Crisp* who had previously won Cheltenham's two-mile Champion Chase by 25 lengths. Similarly, good National form was shown by *Classified* (third in 1986) and *The Tsarevich* (runner-up in 1987), both of whom had been classy two-and-a-half-milers.

Subsequently, however, results have lent scant support to the two-and-a-half-mile theory; and it is noteworthy that the theory was later to be played down by Mercy Rimell, who had helped her husband to train *Gay Trip*. Their winner, she pointed out, had a bit of class and was racing before the major fences were modified in 1990. "It was harder to win a National then", she wrote in her book *Reflections On Racing*. "Jumping was the name of the game. Today you've got to have a horse that stays a lot better because the fences are that much easier, so it's more of a race. Years ago it was a jumping competition. That's the way I look at it. Today your moderate two-and-a-half-mile horse wouldn't have the speed. I'm sure I'm right about that".

Evidence since the fences were modified certainly backs up Mercy Rimell's viewpoint. From 1990 to 2000 the Grand National was dominated by horses with winning form over a distance of at least three miles one furlong, and seven of the ten winners had won or been placed in one of the major non-Aintree Nationals (Irish, Welsh, Scottish and Midlands).

During the 1990s the course was completed by only two runners who had not won beyond two miles five furlongs – *Sure Metal*, 17th in 1996, and 200-1 shot *Back Bar*, 14th in 1999. In 1998 there was strong backing for *Challenger Du Luc*, six times a winner over an extended two and a half miles. Under champion A.P. McCoy, he fell at the first fence.

In 2000 three horses tried to prove the old theory. *Royal Predica* fell at the first and *Red Marauder* fell at the sixth. Most notably, there was *Dark Stranger*, who had impressive form over two and a half miles but had never won over three miles plus. He was made the 9-1 favourite but unseated champion McCoy at the first open ditch.

At last, in 2001, the Grand National was won by a horse seen basically as a middle-distance chaser: *Red Marauder*, a 33-1 shot who had previously scored eight of his nine successes over distances of around two and a half miles or less. Furthermore, third place went to the remounted *Blowing Wind* who had never won beyond two miles and three-and-a-half furlongs.

However, *Red Marauder* had stamina influence through his sire's dam *Precipe Wood*; and the previous September, at Market Rasen, he had scored his first win over three miles. Also this dodgy jumper – a faller at the first Becher's in the 2000 National – was aided by the quagmire conditions at Aintree that resulted in an exceptionally slow place with only two horses finishing without being remounted.

In 2002 McCoy still saw his mount *Blowing Wind* as "an ideal National type"; even though the horse had still never scored beyond two miles and four and a half furlongs, the distance covered when winning the Mildmay of Flete at Cheltenham in the previous month. Despite stamina doubts, the chaser went off the 8-1 favourite and, as one year before, he was a well-beaten third.

Thus, overall, results now strongly support the view that, barring freakishly sluggish ground and numerous fallers, the day of two-and-a-half-milers winning the Grand National are over. Indeed, since 1970 there has not been one National winner who did not have a prior win over three miles or more.

Conclusion: *Do not take a chance on doubtful stayers. Unless exceptionally heavy going prevails, horses with form only over less than three miles are to be eliminated.*

Chapter 8

EXPERIENCE

EXTRAORDINARILY, IN 1887, the 9-2 clear favourite for the Grand National was six-year-old *Spahi* who had not even raced over hurdles let alone fences. He had an excellent record on the Flat, had reportedly schooled brilliantly over fences and had both an outstanding trainer (Henry Linde) and a top rider (Tommy Beasley). Nonetheless, such a short price for an untried novice was absurd; as was the comment of one Irish pundit who wrote: "I never remember so great a steeplechasing certainty". *Spahi* crashed out at the third fence and refused the following year when he reappeared as a 30-1 chance.

This is, of course, a most extreme example of the need for chasing experience before tackling the National. At the same time it should be noted that previous experience over the great Aintree fences is not a prerequisite for success. Scores of horses and riders have been victorious when making their first appearance in the race. In 1859 the winner was *Half Caste*, a six-year-old who had only once before run (and fallen) in a steeplechase. More remarkably, in 1863, five-year-old *Alcibiade* won by a head when making his public debut over fences. That feat was equalled in 1884 by *Voluptuary* whose previous jumping experience had been limited to two hurdle races.

However, that freakish achievement of *Voluptuary* came at a time when there were only 15 starters with nine of them failing to finish. In recent years, to be sure, several National winners have been tuned up in hurdle races before going to Aintree. But the notion of a horse winning the National on his steeplechase debut is now beyond imagination. Newcomers to Aintree might conceivably win but not horses that are relative newcomers to racing over fences. The last horse to win while still a novice was *Mr What* in 1958.

Interestingly, in 2004, veterinary surgeons at the University of Liverpool, led by Chris Proudman, a senior lecturer in equine surgery, studied the fate of all 560 horses in the past 15 Nationals. They concluded that experience counted, with proven stayers being the most likely winners; also that complete novices were twice as likely to fall as those who had stayed the course before, and that even those who had previously tried but fallen fared better than complete beginners. Applying his science before the race, Proudman favoured two old Aintree hands: *Clan Royal* and *Amberleigh House.* His selections finished second and first respectively.

Nevertheless, despite that sensational forecast, the fact remains that overall history does not show that previous experience over the National fences is vital for success. Surprising as it might seem, a marginal majority of Grand National winners (more than 80) were making their first appearance in the race. And only a few of these had previously jumped some of the National fences in other Aintree chases.

Since 1990 twelve of sixteen winners were making their National debut and only three – *Rough Quest* (a faller in the John Hughes Trophy), *Bindaree* (fourth in the John Hughes) and *Monty's Pass* (runner-up in the John Hughes/renamed Topham Trophy) – had encountered the National fences before. Moreover, three winners – *Lord Gyllene* (1997), *Bindaree* (2002) and *Numbersixvalverde* (2006) – were only second season chasers.

Many other horses – among them such greats as *Golden Miller* and *Manifesto* – have fallen in the National and returned to win. However, there have also been many contenders who have shown reluctance to tackle the Aintree fences after a previous bad fall there. And not since *Red Rum's* success in 1977 has the race been won by a previous winner.

Thus it is unproven that horses with previous National experience have a significant advantage. And the same applies to jockeys. Frequently, throughout the race's history, winners have been ridden by newcomers to the challenge, the most recent examples being Paul Carberry (1999), Ruby Walsh (2000) and Niall Madden (2006). In 2003 Leighton Aspell (*Supreme Glory*) and Graham Lee (*Amberleigh House*) finished second and third respectively on their National debut. And amateur Christopher Collins had never even won a race under Rules before finishing third on 50-1 shot *Mr Jones* in the 1965 National.

Conclusion: *No horse should be eliminated simply because it is a newcomer to the Grand National or because it has a rider without experience in the race. But if too many runners remain after following Stage One procedures, eliminate any horse seeking to win the National a second time.*

Chapter 9

FAVOURITES

THE VERY first Aintree Grand National was won by the 5-1 favourite *Lottery*. Overall, however, favourites have a relatively modest record in the race, the worst period for favourites being the years 1928 to 1959 which produced only one successful market leader and, in that instance, a joint 10-1 favourite, *Freebooter* (1950). The first half of the 20th century saw only three clear favourites being first past the post and the second half brought only four.

In almost 80 years since the success of 8-1 *Sprig* in 1927, there have been just five winning clear favourites: *Merryman II* (1960), 13-2; *Grittar* (1962), 7-1; *Rough Quest* (1996), 7-1; *Earth Summit* (1998), 7-1; and *Hedgehunter* (2005), 7-1. Besides *Freebooter*, there was only one other winning joint favourite: *Red Rum*, 9-1 in 1973.

However, analysis of the past eleven Nationals gives a measure of encouragement for favourite backers. Three of the eleven have been won by 7-1 clear favourites, and in one other the clear favourite, *Blowing Wind* (2000) finished third at 8-1. In 2006 each-way backers made a marginal gain as 5-1 joint favourites *Hedgehunter* and *Clan Royal* finished second and third respectively. On the other hand, in four of the eleven races the clear favourite failed to finish. In 2001 three 10-1 co-favourites failed to complete the course; and in 2004 two of three 10-1 co-favourites failed to finish while the other, *Clan Royal*, finished second.

Conclusion: *On the evidence of more recent records there is no longer a case to be made for eliminating favourites per se. See, Chapter 22: Starting Prices.*

Chapter 10

FITNESS

IN 1947, mainland Britain was hit by the severest winter for fifty-three years, with snowdrifts up to 20 ft high and sub-zero temperatures until, in mid-March, the three-month-long big freeze gave way to a thaw that delivered the worst floods in living memory. All racing fixtures between January 22 and March 17 were cancelled and the Cheltenham National Hunt Meeting was postponed until April. Yet, against all odds, the Grand National went ahead on March 29, albeit on heavy, rain-soaked ground.

The great winter hold-up had two major consequences for the National. Because owners had been denied prize-winning opportunities for so long, the race attracted 57 runners, the second largest in history. And, most significantly – in terms of selection – it had been impossible to work a majority of the horses to anywhere near peak fitness.

The result, not so remarkable with the advantage of hindsight, was victory for the eight-year-old Irish outsider *Caughoo*, who had been kept working all winter on the beach of Sutton Strand near Dublin. Yet he went off at 100-1 because his record gave no suggestion of ability to cope with Aintree's fences.

The next severe winter to play havoc with racing in Britain came in 1962–63 when the Thames froze over and snowmen built on Boxing Day were still recognisable in March. Racing on the mainland was put in cold storage for nearly three months, so suggesting another advantage for Irish challengers who had not had their training seriously restricted.

Yet this time, against all expectation, the Irish failed to dominate at either Cheltenham or Aintree. The success of English horses suggested that their trainers had become more adept at finding seashores for work-outs. But, more importantly, racing had been possible in weeks immediately prior to the National on March 30. In near-heavy conditions at Aintree, stamina was at a premium, and victory went to a 66-1 long-shot, *Ayala*, who had had the advantage of two runs in March – falling at Cheltenham but then winning a three-mile chase at Worcester only ten days before the National.

In 2001 the preparation of many horses for the National was interrupted by a foot-and-mouth crisis that resulted in the loss of 57 meetings including the Cheltenham Festival. The epidemic remained such a threat that Aintree racegoers arriving by car had to drive across disinfected mats before parking away from the track, and all had to walk through foot-baths on entering the racecourse.

But, above all, fitness was again put at a premium by quagmire ground conditions so desperate after 16 hours of relentless rain that there was strong support for abandoning the race. Controversially it went ahead, and again there was a shock result, *Red Marauder* winning by a distance at 33-1 and in the slowest time since 1883. There were only four finishers, two of them remounted.

Winning rider and assistant trainer Richard Guest subsequently acknowledged that *Red Marauder* was "probably the worst jumper ever to win a National." Nonetheless, his stamina and fitness were undeniable; and he had profited from being worked in an indoor school furnished with a National-style jump. See, Chapter 7: Distance.

Conclusion: *Today trainers have the advantage of being able to make use of all-weather gallops and indoor facilities. Nevertheless, if freak weather conditions or other circumstances have severely limited racing in February/March, one should be prepared for a relatively shock result; and preference in selection should still be given to horses that have had the benefit of a recent run or an uninterrupted training programme.*

Chapter 11

FOREIGN HORSES

HORSES FROM overseas – that is excluding the never-ending flow of high-class chasers from Ireland – have been seeking Grand National glory since 1856 when two challengers were sent over from France. Many more have followed – from Australia, France, the old Czechoslovakia, Hungary, Japan, New Zealand, Norway, Spain, the former Soviet Union and the United States. But it was not until 1904 that a truly foreign challenger – one not trained in Britain or Ireland – was successful. This was the massive *Moifaa*, New Zealand–bred and owned.

Moifaa succeeded where so many others had failed because he had qualified for a favourable handicap mark by running, albeit without distinction, in three English races. Over and over again, before *Moifaa's* success and since, foreign challengers have been hopelessly anchored on top weight because they were not brought over well in advance to qualify for handicapping purposes.

In 1909, after so many frustrated French entries, one Frenchman got the message: James Hennessy. He gave his five-year-old entire *Lutteur III* time to acclimatise in England and gain experience of English fences in a warm-up steeplechase at Hurst Park, which he won most impressively, just 16 days before going to Aintree. By then, with some allowance for his tender age, he was already reasonably handicapped on 10st. 11lb. He duly won to become the first (and so far only) National winner to be French-owned, bred and ridden.

The next truly foreign success – an all-American one – was achieved in 1938 by *Battleship* who had been shipped over a year and a half in advance to gain experience of English fences and qualify for handicapping. The feat was repeated by US challengers in 1965 and 1980 (See, Chapter 20: Maryland Hunt Cup).

More recently two New Zealand-bred horses have won the National – *Seagram* (1991) and *Lord Gyllene* (1997). But the former had been English-owned and raced since a three-year-old; and the latter, also English-owned and trained, had been running in Britain for the previous two years.

Apart from Ireland, always the source of dangerous challengers, only one overseas country (France) now often has a National contender. Since the 1980s French steeplechasing has flourished anew, most notably spearheaded by the outstanding trainer, Francois Doumen, who burst onto the British racing scene in 1987 when he brought over *Nupsala* to win the King George VI Chase as a 25-1 outsider. He would win the King George four more times, plus the Cheltenham Gold Cup with *The Fellow* (1994). Since then he has regularly had a National entry but so far has achieved nothing better than a seventh place with *Innox* (2005). Meanwhile several French-bred horses have run in the National with distinction (See, Chapter 2: Age), but all had long been trained and exclusively campaigned in England.

In the ten years before 2006 seventy-two French-bred horses ran in the National, with six being placed but none of them winning. Then, in 2006, no fewer than twelve were in the 40-strong line-up. Only one, third-placed *Clan Royal*, completed the course. Remarkably, the fact remains that there has not been a French-bred winner since *Lutteur III* in 1909.

Conclusion: *History shows clearly that any National entry automatically allotted top weight by failing to qualify for handicapping purposes can be safely eliminated. If early procedures have not reduced the field sufficiently, also eliminate any non-Irish foreign horse without previous experience in English chases and, as a final resort, any remaining French-bred horses.*

Chapter 12

FRESHNESS

WHEN *The Lamb* scored his second Grand National victory in 1871 he was racing for the first time in two years. No horse, however, has won on his seasonal debut since 1889 when the Irish mare *Frigate*, a three-times runner-up, triumphed on her first outing for eleven months.

Mely Moss, trained by Charlie Egerton and ridden by Norman Williamson, came nearest to equalling that feat in 2000 when, having his first race for 346 days, he finished runner-up at 25-1 – beaten only a length and a quarter by *Papillon*. A French import, the nine-year-old was having only his sixth race in four seasons since arriving in Britain, though, significantly, he had finished a good second to *Elegant Lord* in the 1999 Fox Hunters at Aintree. *Mely Moss* was raced so rarely because he had famously fragile legs and a tendency to break blood vessels; and in the summer of 2000 he needed a wind operation. Yet remarkably he turned out for the 2001 National – again after a 364-day absence from racing. This time he fell on the first circuit at the Canal Turn, one of eight victims of the pile-up caused by the riderless *Paddy's Return*. There was a slight change in 2002: he went to Aintree after just one seasonal run, 26 days earlier. He came home the last of eleven finishers.

Nowadays, though some horses gain a reputation for "going best fresh", it is generally accepted that a runner should have at least one prep-race, even if it is only over hurdles, before going into the National. Indeed, one has to go back as far as 1898 to find a winner (*Drogheda*) who was without having had a race in the same year. In the 1990s, all nine winners had had races within the 35 previous days. Subsequently all winners have run within the previous 49 days; and all have had between four and six runs since the previous August.

In modern times the overwhelming majority of winners have appeared within three to five weeks of their last race, the most recent exceptions being *West Tip* (1986) after 14 days, *Red Marauder* (2001) after 42 days, and *Hedgehunter* (2005) after 49 days. However, horses have gained a place only two days after their last run: *Irish Lizard*, third in 1953, and *Churchtown Boy*, second to *Red Rum* in 1977. Both ten-year-olds were turning out after winning the Topham Trophy over the National fences.

In the 20th century, winners with the longest lay-off were *Specify* (1971), successful after 84 days' absence, and *Jerry M* (1912) after 76 days. The runner-up who had had the longest break (102 days) was *Durham Edition* (1990). But of all those gaining a place by far the most outstanding horse was dual winner *Manifesto* who, in 1902, at the age of 14, incredibly carried 12st. 8lb. into third place when having his first run for nearly two years.

Conclusion: *Despite the exceptional effort of Mely Moss at the dawn of this century, I favour eliminating any horse without a previous run in the season; and, at Stage Two of the Elimination System any horse without a prep race after the turn of the year.*

Chapter 13

GOING

THE "GOING" – i.e. the state of the ground – is a vital consideration for any punter seeking to make an intelligent pre-race assessment of Grand National runners. According to their particular build and running actions, very few horses are equally effective on both fast and slow ground. To be sure, some may have shown useful form on different sorts of going – firm, good to firm, good, good to soft, soft and heavy – but most are likely to have shown a clear preference and can be eliminated when facing unsuitable conditions. Similarly, horses regarded as uncertain to get the distance may be discounted if they are further disadvantaged by stamina-sapping soft or heavy ground.

By and large, shock results and fewer finishers are most likely to occur when the ground is testing. Since 1962 the official going has been "heavy" five times and on four of those occasions no more than six starters finished. It was muddy going in 1989 when the race was won by *Little Polveir*, who was 7lb. out of the handicap but had proven stamina in winning the Scottish National over boggy ground at Ayr; and the same in 1994 when *Just So*, a renowned mudlark, finished second off a long handicap mark of 8st. 6lb. In similar conditions, in 1998, out-of-the-handicap horses *Samlee* and *St Mellion Fairway* finished third and fourth respectively.

At one time results suggested that older, more experienced horses might be more likely to contend with extremely heavy going. Most notably, in 1962, when the ground was a veritable quagmire, the first three finishers were 12-year-olds. It was heavy in 1980 when 12-year-old *Ben Nevis* won by twenty lengths, with another 12-year-old the third of only four finishers; heavy again in 1989 when 12-year-olds came home first and second. However, all these examples occurred before 1990 when course modifications – most notably the levelling of Becher's treacherous sloping ground on the landing side – were made. Since then only one 12-year-old (*Royal Athlete* at 40-1 in 1995) has triumphed, and that was on good ground.

In 1994 the ground was so wet after heavy rain and snow that some thought the race should not be run. But after the 1993 void National there was added determination to go ahead. The effect on runners was typified by the experience of 6-1 second favourite *Double Silk*, who was cantering until he toppled over at the 13th fence. His rider, Somerset dairy farmer Ron Treloggen, subsequently complained: "His feet literally got stuck in the ground. He had never fallen before".

Sheer stamina, and the masterful handling of Richard Dunwoody, saw 16-1 shot *Miinnehoma*, always moving smoothly on the heavy ground, win by one and a half lengths. Only six completed the course, the last two being 100-1 outsiders.

Again, in 2001, when Aintree took 17mm of rain in 24 hours, there were many who argued that to run would make a mockery of the race. Only four finished (two of them remounted). Significantly, the race was run at such a slow pace that such a dodgy jumper as *Red Marauder* was able to get round, winning in the slowest time since 1883.

Thus, heavy ground is most liable to turn the National into farce; and, though reducing the pace and cushioning falls, it can still be perilous for horses – as shown in 1998 when three suffered fatal falls while all the unseated riders returned unscathed.

Overall, however, jump racing records indicate that horse and rider are in greatest danger when the going is fast. After the debacle of 2001, there was much relief at the advent of drying ground in 2002. But with the going on the fastish side of good the usual cavalry charge resulted in nine starters departing at the first fence, the biggest toll there since 1951.

The lesson was learned. In 2003, after one of the driest months since records began, there was extensive watering of the Aintree course. And on the eve of the National, when the ground was good, the management was prepared to water further if it became any faster. It is now certain that the National will never again be allowed to be run on firm going, as last happened in 1990 when *Mr Frisk* won in record time.

In the circumstances, the punter need no longer be concerned about the possibility of fast ground being liable to cause shock falls early in the race. At the same time, the state of the "going" remains a key factor in pinpointing horses that may be eliminated from the reckoning when selecting horses to be backed. At best, it can result in the largest reduction of prospective candidates for selection.

Very often this step in the elimination process will need to be delayed until the morning of the race if the weather remains uncertain. At other times, most usefully, the state of the "going" is predictable well in advance. This was certainly the case, for example, in 1994.

That year, two months before the race, Nick Mordin presented an ante-post analysis of National entries in the *Weekender*. Of *Just So*, who had finished sixth in the 1992 National at 50-1, he wrote: "In hock deep mud he could get placed at huge odds." And he rightly added, "I can't make the big assumption that he'll get that sort of ground though".

At that time *Just So* (dubbed "Just Slow" by his detractors) was again on offer at 50-1; and those odds were still available on the Thursday before the National when soft or heavy going was already positively assured. That day, memorably, I attended the opening of a new William Hill betting shop in my area. Conducting the proceedings in his usual flamboyant style was racing pundit John McCririck.

In those days, though he himself would deny it, McCririck was capable of influencing market moves by his loud pronouncements. For weeks before the National he was extolling the merits of *Master Oats*, and by giving his fancy the full TV-hype treatment he certainly contributed to the horse's odds shortening from 40-1 to 8-1.

At the opening of the betting shop McCririck was still proclaiming *Master Oats* as "a good thing." Subsequently, he asked the gathered punters which horses they were backing in the National. In my case, I replied that I did not have one favoured selection but suggested that the 50-1 for *Just So* was outstanding each-way value. No one voiced agreement.

Subsequently, John Budden of *The Sporting Life* observed in his Grand National guide that *Just So* "would be strongly favoured if the National were run over six miles". But so heavy was the ground that it was going to feel more like six miles, and, sure enough, in a pulsating finish, *Just So* came home second at 20-1, beaten only a length-and-a-half by *Miinnehoma*, with 5-1 favourite *Moorcroft Boy* twenty lengths back in third place. *Master Oats*, a faller, was one of five horses to exit at the 13th fence.

It was the slowest National since 1955. But although I had a small each-way "fun bet" on *Just So* at 50-1, this could not be claimed as a triumph for the Elimination Method. Being 22lb. out of the handicap proper, *Just So* did not qualify for system selection, and the same applied to third-placed *Moorcroft Boy* and the so fancied *Master Oats*, both also in the long handicap.

However, following my elimination of all horses running from out of the handicap, only thirteen runners had remained. These were reduced to ten by dismissing *Quirinus* as an automatically top-weighted Czech entry; *Young Hustler* as a seven-year-old; and *The Fellow* because he was reappearing only 23 days after winning the Cheltenham Gold Cup.

The extremely heavy going was now a valuable aid to reducing the field still further. Out went *Black Humour* and *Topsham Bay* who had never won on worse than good to soft, and *Romany King* who had won on soft but only over a distance of 2 miles 2 furlongs. The rest were proven stayers, but I still needed to lose one more for my maximum of six selections. So finally I dispensed with *Ebony Jane* on the grounds that a mare had not won the National since 1951.

An unfortunate choice. This was to be the third successive National that a saw a mare running into a place, *Ebony Jane* finishing fourth at 25-1. Happily, however, the six selected for equal each-way backing included

Miinnehoma, and with odds of 16-1 a reasonable profit was assured.

Conclusion: *Noting horses clearly disadvantaged by the state of the "going" is of paramount importance in the elimination process. If there is any danger of the ground conditions changing on the day of the National, delay making final selections for as long as may be necessary.* See, Chapter 27: The System in Action.

Chapter 14

GREYS

IN THE entire history of the Grand National, only two greys have ever won the race: *The Lamb* (1868 and 1871) and *Nicolaus Silver* (1961). And very few have even finished in a place. This overwhelmingly dismal record might seem reason enough to eliminate any grey entered from the race. However, one should bear in mind that greys are in a distinct minority with only about three per cent of racehorses qualifying for that description.

On the other hand, in the early years of the National, greys were not so uncommon as today. When the mare *Charity* triumphed in 1841, a year with merely eleven runners, two well-backed greys, *Cigar* and *Peter Simple*, were beaten by only one length and one and a half lengths respectively. The latter was third again in 1842 and runner-up by two lengths in 1845.

Even so, it was almost three decades before a grey was successful in the race; and after the dual triumphs of *The Lamb* another 90 years before one scored again. In those nine decades, greys rarely made any impression at Aintree, the best being the six-year-old *Downpatrick*, third in 1880 and fourth in 1883.

In 1930, for the first (and only) time two greys – *Glangesia* and *Gate Book* – led the National field, staying in front beyond Becher's first time round. But the latter fell soon after while 33-1 shot *Glangesia* went on to be the fourth of six finishers, and came back to be seventh in 1931. The grey *Kilnagory* was eighth in a field of 57 starters in 1947.

The miserable record of greys finally ended in 1961 when *Nicolaus Silver* was a worthy five-lengths winner at 28-1. But in the next 35 years only two greys finished in a place – *The Beeches*, fourth in 1969, and *Loving Words*, third in 1982 after being remounted. The latter had been unlucky in being badly hampered by two fallers at the last open ditch where his rider was unseated.

By now there was a growing superstition that greys were somehow doomed for failure at Aintree – a belief highlighted in 1987 by the fatal fall of beautiful *Dark Ivy*, the 11-2 second favourite, and strengthened in 1988 when Jenny Pitman's *Smith's Man* broke down after the first fence and the only other grey in the race, *Brass Change*, fell at the third last.

Of course, the record of greys might have been more impressive but for the fact that some outstanding grey chasers – most notably *Desert Orchid* and *One Man* – have been loved too much to be risked in the roughhouse of the National. *Desert Orchid* was, in fact, entered by his trainer one year and was duly allotted a massive 12st. 2lb. Immediately there was a public outcry at the possibility of this national treasure competing, and he was promptly withdrawn.

Thereafter, the failure of greys in the National continued. Unusually, in 1993, three greys were in the confused line-up. But this was the National declared void after an uncontrolled false start. One grey, *Stay On Tracks*, was correctly pulled up after the first circuit. The other two, *Farm Week* and *Howe Street*, fell at the 4th and 20th fences respectively. In 1995 the Irish grey *Desert Lord* fell at the 21st.

Talk of a "grey hoodoo" was revived the following year when *Son Of War*, winner of the 1994 Irish National, was all the rage at Aintree, the most napped horse in the race and hugely fancied at 8-1 to end a long losing run of Irish horses. All season he had been laid out for the challenge. But on the day he was no match for the favourite *Rough Quest* and was in tenth place when he unseated Conor O'Dwyer at the 24th (Canal Turn).

In more recent years, however, greys in the National have won considerable respect – a change due in no small measure to the influence of *Roselier*, the grey stallion who was the sire of such useful greys as *Suny Bay*, *Senor El Bettruti*, *Baronet* and *Kendal Cavalier*, as well as such strong non-grey National contenders as *Royal Athlete*, *Moorcroft Boy* and *Ebony Jane*.

The greatest of these greys was *Suny Bay*. In 1997 he finished second – albeit 25 lengths behind runaway leader *Lord Gyllene*. The following year, six days after being fifth in the Cheltenham Gold Cup, he ran at Aintree carrying 12st., so giving at least 10lb. to all his rivals and two stone to 30 in the 37-strong field. Remarkably, he again finished runner-up – this time beaten eleven lengths by *Earth Summit* who had a 23lb. advantage. *Timeform* commented: "In form terms this was the best performance in the race over 20 years and one of the best in the modern era".

Next, most significantly, came the performances of greys in the 2002 National. Unusually, five appeared in the 40-strong line-up: *Kingsmark*, *What's Up Boys*, *Carryonharry*, *Gun 'N Roses* and *Birkdale*; and remarkably three were among the eleven finishers and two of these were placed. Outstanding was the run of *What's Up Boys*, the Hennessy Cognac Gold Cup winner, who had been a staying-on fifth in the Cheltenham Gold Cup only three weeks earlier. Now, carrying 11st. 6lb., he led on the run-in, only to be headed in the last 75 yards, beaten a mere length and three-quarters by *Bindaree* to whom he was conceding 16lb. *Kingsmark*, who had fallen only once in 17 chases, finished well back in fourth place.

On their reappearance in 2004 *What's Up Boys* and *Kingsmark* were again both heavily weighted. The former was brought down at the 6th, the latter was the ninth of eleven finishers, and the only other grey in the race, *Royal Atalza*, was pulled up two out. In 2005, *Double Honour* and *Marcus Du Berlais* unseated their riders on the second circuit, while the third grey in the field – 9-1 second favourite *Strong Resolve* – was a disappointing 17th of 21 finishers. In 2006, the only grey, *Ross Comm*, fell at the fourth fence.

Conclusion: *In the light of more recent runs, and despite that dismal record of only three National wins, it now remains clear on the evidence of the 2002 race that grey contenders are no longer to be readily dismissed on grounds of colour alone.*

Chapter 15

HANDICAPPING

THE BRITISH Horseracing Authority, having recently taken over from the British Horseracing Board (BHB) as the governing authority of British Racing, maintains a list of official ratings (0 to 175) for every National Hunt horse; and these, revised weekly to take into account latest performances, are the primary basis for determining handicap weights. The higher the rating the higher the weight to be carried, with each extra point on the scale being the equivalent of an extra pound. However, in the case of the Grand National, the official handicapper may, at his own discretion, choose not to rely solely on ratings but also allow for the "Aintree factor" – i.e. giving extra weight to horses with good past form over the National fences.

The system is further confused by the fact that the National weights are framed in February, two months in advance of the race; and they remain fixed irrespective of any subsequent revision of the ratings. No weight is added as a penalty for a horse scoring a win during the two-month run-up to the big race. Thus, controversially, an entered horse may fail to make the line-up limited to 40 runners even though he has since acquired a rating higher than one or more of those who have successfully made the cut.

Those horses given a weight below the National minimum of 10st. are described as being "in the long handicap" or "out of the handicap proper". If, at the five-day or overnight declaration stage, the horse with the maximum top weight is withdrawn, the next horse in the pecking order is raised to that level and all others are raised by the same margin. When this happens, it is possible that a horse below the 10st. mark may be brought into the handicap proper.

In 1960 a minimum rating of 120 was introduced for horses to qualify for the National – a measure taken after the fate of horses totally unsuited to the demands of Aintree had brought the race into disrepute. But in 1996 the National had only 27 runners from 82 entries, the smallest field since 1960, and the BHB responded by lowering the qualification by 10lb. – i.e. reducing the minimum rating to 110. Many more horses became eligible for entry and since the turn of the century the safety limit of 40 runners has been easily achieved.

Over the years, however, the rating needed to make the line-up has steadily risen – evidence of the improved quality of the race with its greatly increased prize-money. In 2003 the senior jumps handicapper Phil Smith said he would be surprised if the main rating in the line-up was ever less than 130. And, indeed, by 2005, a horse needed to be rated 134 to get a run. That year, for the first time, and again in 2006, the whole field was in the handicap proper – i.e. running off their correct marks.

Such was the rise in quality that in 2006 the average rating of the 148 entries was, at 135, the highest it had ever been – a record due to the fact that a huge number were in the 140 to 145 range, with 14 horses having official ratings of 150 or higher. It is noteworthy, however, that the past ten winners have been officially rated between 136 and 149, a narrow band suggesting that the victor is most likely to be a horse with a touch of class but not among the highest weights.

The handicap has long been recognised as a major factor to be considered in trying to determine the Grand National winner. For example, prior to *Lord Gyllene's* success in 1997, there had been only three winners from "out of the handicap" in the past 30 years – *Foinavon* (in freak circumstances) in 1967, *Rubstic* in 1979 and *Little Polveir* in 1989.

During this period there was a strong case to be made in favour of limiting one's selections to horses in the handicap proper. Indeed, throughout the 1980s and 1990s it was my custom to eliminate all horses not in the handicap proper. To be sure, this resulted in shock losses on three occasions – in 1989, 1997 and 1999. But overall it was a hugely profitable ploy.

Most notably the method netted *Last Suspect*, the 50-1 winner in 1985; and it was especially effective in 1990 when there were just eleven horses in the handicap proper and, most unusually, good to firm going. Of these, *Bonanza Boy*, *Hungary Hur* and *Gainsay* could be eliminated as being unsuited by the going. Out, too, went *West Tip* as a 13-year-old; *Call Collect* as a Cheltenham winner only three weeks earlier; and *Pukha Major* who had an aversion to starting and no form to commend him. Only five remained to be backed each-way: *Mr Frisk* (the 16-1 winner), *Durham Edition* (second at 9-1), *Brown Windsor* (fourth at 7-1), *Joint Sovereignty* (unseated rider, 19th) and *Bob Tisdall* (the last of twenty finishers).

It all seemed so easy. But one year later it was never more difficult. In 1991, I faced an impossible situation with no fewer than nineteen horses, almost half of the field, being in the handicap proper – too many to cover all those who qualified after applying other elimination factors. For the first time in years I admitted defeat and settled for backing just one selection each-way. I chose *Docklands Express* because of his remarkable consistency: he had had fourteen races over fences, winning eight of them and never finishing out of the first three. Also, like the previous year's winner, he was trained by Kim Bailey.

The result was just the kind of disappointment that I normally seek to avoid by following a method that usually gives five or six chances of success. My betting interest in this National ended with the fall of *Docklands Express* at the very first fence. Afterwards his young rider, Anthony Tory, a newcomer to the race, said, "He had never jumped over a drop fence before and it found him out".

Happily it was back to business as usual in the relatively easy years of 1992, 1994 and 1995. In 1992 only eleven horses were in the handicap proper and from these my six selections included the winner *Party Politics* and runner-up *Romany King*. In 1994, with just thirteen in the handicap proper, I had only one of my "super six" in the frame, but happily that was *Miinnehoma*, the 16-1 winner. Best of all, in 1995, with only eleven running off their true handicap mark, my bets covered the 40-1 winner *Royal Athlete* and *Dubacilla*, placed fourth at 9-1.

But times were a-changing. There were signs that the chances of out-of-the-handicap horses had improved since 1990 with the softening of Aintree's most formidable fences. In 1994, given heavy going, the mudlark *Just So* had been second off a long handicap mark of 8st. 6lb.; and *Encore Un Peu* was a close runner-up in 1996 when running from 9lb. out of the handicap, with *Sir Peter Lely* and *Three Brownies*, even lower rated, finishing fourth and sixth respectively. The following year the victorious *Lord Gyllene* was 1lb. out of the handicap proper.

Finally, the situation changed most dramatically in 1999 following the appointment of Mr Smith, a former maths teacher, to succeed long-serving Christopher Mordaunt as the BHB's senior jumps handicapper. He was given three briefs in respect of the Grand National: to get more entries, to attract the best horses possible – and to get more horses in the handicap proper.

All those aims would be achieved within five years, and results soon indicated how influential he was in reshaping the race. In 1999, most unusually, both the winner (*Bobbyjo*) and the runner-up (*Blue Charm*) were running from out of the handicap. Moreover, unprecedented in modern times, the winner was a full stone out of the handicap.

Subsequently, the number of runners in the handicap proper rose to 17 in 2001, 31 in 2002, 33 in 2003, and 36 in 2004. Finally, in 2005, there was the unprecedented circumstance of all 40 National starters running off 10st. 5lb. or more. Alas, long since gone were the days when, most valuably, the elimination method could be advanced by taking out horses carrying more than their allotted weight to meet the National's 10st. minimum.

Nevertheless, the work of the official handicapper still merits careful examination in the selection process. For example, in 2005, to make the race even more competitive, Mr Smith applied the "Aintree factor". Also, learning from experience, he said he was no longer to be fooled by the successful Irish ploy of having a horse "naff around over hurdles" to protect its handicap mark.

But his actions hardly matched his words. In the 2004 National, *Hedgehunter* had held the lead from the 10th until the 29th where he was headed by *Clan Royal*. He seemed certain of a place until, coming to the last, he fell for the first time in his career. It was a most promising Aintree debut, and yet, in 2005, Mr Smith allotted the Irish chaser 10st. 12lb. – no more than he had carried the previous year.

Significantly, prior to the framing of the weights in 2005, *Hedgehunter* had run in five hurdle races to avoid a rise in the ratings. Once he had been given his National weight he promptly made his seasonal debut over fences and won well. Later, following withdrawals, the National weights were raised 3lb. but it made no difference since all the runners were now in the handicap proper. *Hedgehunter*, romped home by fourteen lengths as 7-1 favourite – the first horse in 17 years to carry 11st. or more to victory.

Again, in 2006, Mr Smith managed to compress the weights to make the race more open, without a single horse running from out of the handicap. But again a few of his judgements were open to question. Following the new fashion, several leading contenders, including *Clan Royal* and *Numbersixvalverde*, had been campaigned over hurdles to protect their handicap mark. And most notably he appeared to have let *Clan Royal* off lightly with an initial weight of 10st. 8lb. – three pounds less than the previous year when, leading the field, the gelding was unluckily taken out by a loose horse at the second Becher's.

The handicapper explained that *Clan Royal* "left the

race too far out last year for me to make a judgment as to where he would have finished." But, bearing in mind that he had been the three-length runner-up to *Amberleigh House* in 2004, there was every reason to suppose that he would have finished strongly in contention. Thus, when the weights were announced, he was the unanimous favourite with the major firms.

Going off as 5-1 joint favourite, *Clan Royal* finished third behind *Numbersixvalverde* and his co-market leader *Hedgehunter*. The latter, with an official rating of 156, was a most creditable runner-up under a top weight of 11st. 12lb. But the winner, and indeed eight of the nine finishers, were within the rating range of 136 and 142. The last horse to win on a mark above 149 was *Rough Quest*, rated 152 in 1996, the year with only 27 runners.

Conclusion: *Although this century has not yet seen a National winner emerging from "out of the handicap", I no longer choose to eliminate such runners automatically but only as a last resort. Meanwhile, it is now evident that special attention needs to be paid to leading contenders who have protected their handicap mark by running over hurdles – and especially if they have an official rating between 136 and 149.* See, Chapter 25: Weights.

Chapter 16

IRISH HORSES

IRISH HORSES have appeared regularly in the Grand National ever since the first running in 1839 when owner Tom Ferguson brought over three contenders. It was not until 1847 that the Irish successfully plundered the race, piling their money on the lightly-weighted Coolreagh-bred *Matthew*, the 10-1 joint favourite. Four years later little Irish-bred *Abd-El-Kader* became the first horse to win successive Nationals. And since then Irish horses have triumphed at Aintree to a truly astonishing degree.

Significantly, though many were English-owned and trained, a majority of Grand National winners have been Irish-bred; and these include the greatest – *Red Rum*, the only triple winner; *Golden Miller*, the only horse to achieve the Cheltenham Gold Cup–National double; *Manifesto*, eight times a contender, scoring his second win under a massive 12st. 7lb.; *Cloister*, the first to win by forty lengths and with that same maximum weight; *Jerry M*, equally burdened; and the dual Cheltenham Gold Cup winner *L'Escargot*.

It was from the Emerald Isle that the greatest Irish wizard of them all, Michael Vincent O'Brien, having won three consecutive Gold Cups and three successive Champion Hurdles, uniquely sent over three successive Grand National winners: *Early Mist* (1953), *Royal Tan* (1954) and *Quare Times* (1955).

However, there have been notable lulls in Ireland's

triumphs at Aintree. In 1939, *Workman* was the first Irish-bred, owned and trained winner since *Troytown* in 1920. And when *L'Escargot* beat *Red Rum* in 1975 he was becoming the first Irish-trained winner since *Mr What* in 1958. Then came an even longer period – almost a quarter of a century – without an Irish success.

Everything changed in 1999 when the 24-year drought was ended by the victory of *Bobbyjo*. The following year brought the win of *Papillon*; and when *Monty's Pass* triumphed in 2003 it meant that Ireland had had three National winners in five years – all of them from relatively small yards. The score became five winners in eight years with the success of *Hedgehunter* (2005) and *Numbersixvalverde* (2006). In the latter year no fewer than 21 of the 40 runners in the National were Irish-bred, taking four of the first five places. And only by a short head did Ireland fail to equal their recent 1-2-3 clean sweep in the Cheltenham Gold Cup.

The great Irish revival can partly be explained by the cunning of trainers in running challengers over hurdles to protect their handicap mark. Primarily, however, the explanation lies in hard economics. In times of far greater prosperity, there are now plenty of well-heeled Irish owners who can resist offers from across the water. In addition, Irish racing has had the advantage of government subsidies, greatly aiding racecourses, raising prize-money and providing tax exemptions for home-based jockeys and very generous tax concessions for stud owners.

In 2006, after Irish horses were the first three home in the Cheltenham Gold Cup, Michael O'Leary, owner of the winning *War of Attrition*, explained his country's dominance most succinctly: "Because we're keeping all the good horses at home and selling you guys (British owners) all the rubbish". Thus, gone are the days when leading trainers in England could readily plunder the great equine resources of Ireland – e.g. Jenny Pitman's inspired shopping spree of 1986, buying four unbroken three-year-olds – *Royal Athlete*, *Garrison Savannah*, *Esha Ness* and *Willsford* no less.

Furthermore, barring an extraordinary economic recession, Ireland will continue to be a major force in National Hunt racing because, beyond Britain, no other country is so successful in breeding jumpers and has so many events for hurdlers and chasers. Twenty-four of its 27 courses are used for jumping as well as flat racing, with only the Curragh being used exclusively for the Flat.

Conclusion: *Leading Irish contenders are to be scrutinised very carefully, having special regard for horses that have been artfully run over hurdles to protect their handicap mark.*

Chapter 17

JOCKEYS

IT IS generally accepted by National Hunt jockeys that, however talented a rider may be, he or she can only win the Grand National if on the right horse – the "right horse" being the one that performs best on the day without inadvertently suffering a mishap. Quite simply, the National is no respecter of reputations, with luck in the running remaining a prerequisite of great and moderate riders alike.

Since 1900, Grand National winners have been ridden by only 14 jockeys who have, at some time, been holders of the National Hunt jockey championship. Champion riders who have been denied National victory include Peter Scudamore (eight times title-holder), John Francome (seven titles), Billy Stott and Tim Molony (five), Fred Rimell and Josh Gifford (four), Stan Mellor and Terry Biddlecombe (three), Ron Barry and Jonjo O'Neill (two) and one-time champions Jack Dowdeswell, Dick Francis and Tim Brookshaw.

Most remarkably, A.P. McCoy, the most successful jockey of all time, who has been champion every year since 1995–96 and who rode his 2,500th winner in 2006, continues to pursue his first National win.

Five times he has been the top jockey at the Aintree meeting, but in eleven attempts at the big one he has frustratingly been limited to three third places and eight non-finishes.

Of jockeys who have ridden 1,000 or more winners

in British National Hunt racing, the most successful in the Grand National is Richard Dunwoody, who scored on *West Tip* (1986) and *Miinnehoma* (1994). Since then two other jockeys – Carl Llewellyn and Ruby Walsh – have scored a second National win but there has been no third-time winning jockey since Brian Fletcher repeated his success on *Red Rum* in 1974.

In recent years, leading jockeys in Ireland have had an excellent record at Aintree. However, Frank Berry, ten times champion rider in Ireland and winner of the 1972 Cheltenham Gold Cup on *Glencaraig Lady*, rode in eight Nationals and never finished better than in seventh place, on *The Ellier* (1987).

Conclusion: *The fame of a jockey is not to be taken into consideration when seeking to eliminate runners.* See, Chapter 8: Experience.

Chapter 18

LADY RIDERS

THE SIGHT of Elizabeth Taylor (as 14-year-old Velvet Brown) winning the Grand National in the 1944 Hollywood film of Enid Bagnold's best-selling novel, *National Velvet*, has aroused dreams of Aintree glory in countless lady riders. Yet it was not until late 1971 that the Jockey Club agreed that women could compete under Rules in Britain, and not until 1976, when the Sex Discrimination Act came into effect, that women were allowed to ride under National Hunt Rules.

Since then fourteen women have ridden in the Grand National and in a total of seventeen attempts just four have completed the course: Geraldine Rees, the last of eight finishers on *Cheers* (66-1) in 1982; Rosemary Henderson, fifth on her *Fiddlers Pike* (100-1) in 1994; Carrie Ford, fifth on her *Forest Gunner* (8-1) in 2005; and Nina Carberry, the last of nine finishers on *Forest Gunner* (33-1) in 2006.

Throughout the 1980s there remained enormous prejudice against lady riders, with Colonel Blimps arguing that women were simply not physically strong enough to compete in the race. And it was reflected in the betting that sent off three female-ridden challengers at 200-1 and one (a first fence faller) priced at 500-1.

Not only male chauvinists dismissed the possibility of a woman riding the National winner. In 1990 the famed lady trainer Mercy Rimell wrote in *Reflections on Racing*: "I don't approve of women riding in open professional races under Rules. They are not strong enough". And in 1993, jump jockey Steve Smith Eccles wrote in his autobiography, *The Last of the Cavaliers*: "Bluntly, I have never yet seen a girl jump jockey who is any better than a third-rate man. In general, they are more of a nuisance than a virtue and, because they will never compete on my terms, I would prefer if they were not riding at all."

But one year later the 1994 National saw a truly extraordinary challenge by a lady rider: Rosemary Henderson, popularly dubbed "the Galloping Granny", though, in fact, she had no children. She was, at 51, the oldest rider in the race and her horse, 13-year-old *Fiddlers Pike* – on whom she had won the Warwick National and the John Hughes National Trial at Chepstow in the previous season – was also the oldest in a 36-strong field.

Standing tall in her irons, Mrs Henderson handled her 100-1 no-hoper brilliantly, taking all the fences neatly and finishing the fifth of only six riders to complete the course. After fifteen National starts by lady riders, she had set a new standard for her sex, significantly riding a horse she owned and trained.

Yet a whole decade passed before another lady rider appeared; and for the first time such a challenge was taken very seriously indeed. Carrie Ford was riding *Forest Gunner*, trained by her husband, and she had already won with him over the National fences, in the 2004 Foxhunters' Chase, just ten weeks after giving birth to a daughter. The 11-year-old gelding was allotted a place in the handicap proper and incredibly went off as the 8-1 second favourite.

Bookmakers claimed that a *Forest Gunner* win

would cost them a staggering £100 million. In the end, as feared, he just did not quite stay and was unable to maintain the pace from two out. But Carrie, only 5ft 3in. tall, gave him a faultless ride and they finished five places ahead of the previous year's winner, *Amberleigh House*, whose trainer "Ginger" McCain had threatened to bare his bum if a lady rode the winner.

Mrs Ford's performance showed clearly that the outright dismissal of lady jump jockeys hardly bears credence in an age when women can outclass men in the most hazardous equine sport of eventing; when a woman is strong enough, mentally and physically, to sail round the world in the fastest-ever single-handed time; and when women conquer Mount Everest, row solo across the Atlantic, and run the marathon in times once considered beyond the capability of men.

This was further demonstrated the following year when 21-year-old Nina Carberry also completed the course on *Forest Gunner* – in the process bettering brother Paul who had fallen on *Sir OJ* at the second Becher's. Never had a lady rider had stronger credentials for success in the National. Her pedigree was outstanding: a maternal grandfather (Dan Moore) who had missed Grand National victory by a mere head on *Royal Danieli* in 1938 and had trained the 1975 winner, *L'Escargot*; a father (Tom) who had ridden that winner; a brother (Paul) who had triumphed in 1999 on *Bobbyjo*, trained by their father.

Growing up with five brothers, Nina had developed into a rider able to compete with the best of horsemen. In 2005 she became the first woman to win a professional race at the Cheltenham Festival since Gee Armytage in 1987. The following year Mick Fitzgerald observed:

"She doesn't ride like a girl"; and even the great A.P. McCoy acknowledged, "For a girl she's exceptional".

In the 2006 National, she had no real chance on *Forest Gunner*, now a 12-year-old who chased the leaders until fading from four out. But given the right horse, here surely was a lady rider equipped to make Velvet Brown a reality.

Conclusion: *In 1988, as one of three lady riders in the race, Gee Armytage said: "It is only a matter of time before a woman rides the winner of the National. It's all about having the right horse and that all-important slice of luck." Realistically, it could be a long time since there are so few lady jump jockeys and, in general, owners and trainers still favour male riders. But basically I agree. It is all about having the right horse and – provided the jockey has proven form in chases – no horse should be eliminated solely because it has a lady rider.*

Chapter 19

MARES

IN NEARLY 160 runnings the Grand National has been won by a mare on only thirteen occasions and not once since the somewhat fortuitous success of 40-1 shot *Nickel Coin* in 1951. In 1958 *Tibretta* was a distant second and in 1970 *Miss Hunter* finished third, a place also gained by *Eyecatcher* in 1976 and 1977. But thereafter mares made no impression in the race until 1991 when *Auntie Dot* came home third at 50-1.

In the light of this dismal record – not a single winning mare in the past 56 years – there might seem to be an overwhelming case for eliminating any mare in a Grand National line-up. However, plenty of excuses can be made for this poor showing; not least the fact that the mares are at a numerical disadvantage. Very often well-bred mares with promising racing form will be retired by the age of four to be mated with a stallion standing at stud. Thus, overall in modern times, geldings running in the Grand National have outnumbered mares by more than 50 to 1.

Then, again, there is the nagging suspicion that a mare, by virtue of coming into season every three weeks in spring and summer, is all the more likely to have an off-day – i.e. a fit of temperament known as "being marish" – just when peak condition matters. And, of course, the National falls more or less at the beginning of spring.

Furthermore, there have been cases of mares being

victims of sexual harassment. A classic example occurred in 1937 when *Cooleen* might conceivably have won the National if, all the way from the Canal Turn, she had not been continually attacked, sometimes savagely, by the riderless 100-1 shot *Drim*. In the circumstances, jockey Jack Fawcus worked wonders to bring her home in second place, three lengths behind *Royal Mail*, with another mare, *Pucka Belle*, a further ten lengths back in third. *Cooleen* returned to finish fourth in the next two Nationals.

If we look back to the 19th century, when mares were more commonly run, there is plenty of evidence that they can be every bit as tough and competitive as their male rivals. And in the 1880s *Frigate* became the most consistent mare in Grand National history – seven times a contender and three times finishing second before winning at the sixth attempt.

Nevertheless, when *Sheila's Cottage* won in 1948 she was the first successful mare for 46 years; and for 40 years after *Nickel Coin's* victory in 1951 the record of mares remained abysmal, with only three – *Tibretta*, *Miss Hunter* and *Eyecatcher* – running in the National with a measure of distinction.

But this case against mares needs to be reviewed following their improved performance since 1990 when modifications blunted the sharpest edge of the most formidable Aintree fences. Subsequently there came a remarkable change of fortune with mares finishing in a place in four successive Nationals: *Auntie Dot* (1991), third at 50-1; *Laura's Beau* (1992), third at 12-1; *Ebony Jane* (1994), fourth at 25-1; and *Dubacilla* (1995), fourth at 9-1.

Dubacilla's short odds reflected how prejudice

against mares had greatly diminished. Indeed, in 1999, there was the extraordinary development of a mare (*Fiddling The Facts*) going off as the 6-1 National favourite. Unfortunately she had no luck in the running and was brought down with four other fallers at the second Becher's.

Conclusion: *Only two mares have appeared in the past nine Grand Nationals – evidence of the reluctance of trainers to risk mares in the hurly-burly of the most gruelling handicap steeplechase. One (Wicked Crack) was a faller at the first in 2002, the other (six-year-old L'Aventure) was the 15th of 21 finishers in 2005. But on the evidence of performances in the early 1990s mares can no longer be dismissed solely by reason of their sex.*

Chapter 20

MARYLAND HUNT CUP

THE PREMIER steeplechase of the United States, inaugurated in 1894, is run over four miles and 22 formidable upright timbers at Far Hills, Maryland. It has provided the most valuable guide to the strength of American challengers for Grand National glory.

Ten-year-old *Billy Barton*, a 33-1 chance, was the first Maryland Hunt Cup winner to make an impression at Aintree, being the only other finisher (remounted) when *Tipperary Tim* won the chaotic National of 1928. Next came *Jay Trump* who, after twice winning the Maryland, won the 1965 National by three-quarters of a length. Similarly, 12-year-old *Ben Nevis* was a dual winner of the Hunt Cup before scoring a 20 lengths victory in the 1980 National.

After a ten-year gap there was another contender for the Maryland–National double: the quietly fancied *Uncle Merlin* who, like *Ben Nevis*, was sent over to be trained by Tim Forster. To my shame, I automatically eliminated this nine-year-old even though he had a three times National-winning trainer and a National-winning jockey, Hywel Davies. He was carrying 15lb. more than his allotted weight and at that time I discarded all horses running from out the handicap proper.

I was lucky to get away with it and land the first, second and fourth finishers in my five selections. *Uncle Merlin* jumped superbly well and – in the fastest ever National – he led the record-breaking *Mr Frisk* for 22 fences. Then he was desperately unfortunate to be put out of the race by one error when he was heading the field at the second Becher's.

Eight years later another dual Maryland Hunt Cup winner – *Buck Jakes* – was sent to Tim Forster to be prepared for the National. This big (17.2) grey had scored eleven timber-race wins for trainer Charlie Fenwick, the American who had partnered *Ben Nevis*, one of Forster's three National winners. Moreover, he had smashed *Ben Nevis's* course record by winning his first Maryland Cup in 8 min. 30.6 sec.; and he had twice won the American Grand National Timber Stakes.

Here, it seemed, was an outstanding candidate to become the fourth American chaser to win the National. Greedily, for the first and last time, I succumbed to the temptation to take full advantage of attractive ante-post odds of 50-1. As planned, *Buck Jakes* qualified for a handicap mark by having three runs in Britain. Unfortunately, those three runs produced a dismal 4PP and subsequently he was withdrawn from the National and duly retired. Lesson learned.

Conclusion: *No Maryland Hunt Cup winner making it to the Aintree line-up is to be lightly eliminated if meeting the outlined requirements regarding age, weight and suitable going.*

Chapter 21

POINTERS

NO SINGLE race in Britain and Ireland stands out as a truly reliable guide to the prospect of horses entered for the Grand National. And, as noted earlier, Cheltenham Festival form has not been very useful – only one horse (*Seagram*, 1991) in the last 45 years winning there immediately prior to National success, and *Rough Quest* (1996) being exceptional in having been placed in the Gold Cup before winning the National a few weeks later.

However, rightly or wrongly, certain races are regarded as useful pointers. The earliest of these is the Hennessy Cognac Gold Cup, a highly prestigious handicap test of staying chasers run over three miles two-and-a-half furlongs at Newbury in November. Here it is placed horses, rather than winners, that have fared best in the National.

In the 1960s three Hennessy winners failed at Aintree. *Springbok* (1962) finished fifth as the 10-1 favourite in the 1963 National. *Rondetto* (1967) fell in the 1968 National, finished third in 1969, and unseated his rider in 1970. *Spanish Steps* (1969) was a latecomer to the National, finishing fourth in 1973 and 1974, then third in 1975. On the other hand, two Hennessy winners have since come close to scoring at Aintree. *Suny Bay*, who won at Newbury in 1997 after being runner-up in that year's National, was runner-up again in 1998 when giving a massive 23lb. to the winner, *Earth Summit*.

In 2002, another grey, *What's Up Boys*, made a most gallant bid to achieve the Hennessy–National double, going down by only one-and-three-quarter lengths to *Bindaree*, who had been fifth in the Hennessy and now had a 16lb. advantage in the weights.

Horses placed in the Hennessy have fared better. They include *Aldaniti*, third in 1977, and winning the National four years later; *Mr Frisk*, third in 1989 and winning the National the following year; *Party Politics*, a good second ahead of *Docklands Express* before his Aintree success in 1992, with *Docklands Express*, the favourite, finishing fourth; and *Rough Quest*, second at Newbury before going on to win the 1996 National in which *Superior Finish*, third in the Hennessy, was third again.

Red Marauder, like *Bindaree*, had been fifth in the Hennessy before his National victory in 2001. *Hedgehunter* was fourth in the 2003 Hennessy, two years before winning the National. And not to be forgotten is the so unlucky *Freddie*, who had been second to the mighty *Arkle* in the 1965 Hennessy. Earlier that year he had been beaten by only three-quarters of a length in the National, and he was second again at Aintree in 1966.

Of all the British courses, Haydock Park is regarded as providing an especially useful preparation for the National since, like Aintree, it is left-handed, reasonably flat, with not dissimilar drop fences, open ditches and a water jump. A number of horses – among them *Sheila's Cottage*, *Russian Hero* and *Freebooter* (in successive years) – have won there before going on to victory at Aintree. And, most tellingly, *Red Rum* ran there on each of his last outings before making his five National appearances.

In more recent years, however, Haydock form has proved less useful. Most notably, the Greenalls Grand

National Trial (renamed the Red Square Vodka Gold Cup), run there in February over an extended three and a half miles, was won in 1997 by *Suny Bay* who went on to finish runner-up in the next two Grand Nationals.

Four handicap chases are run at Aintree over one circuit of the National course and therefore at least provide a guide to ability to cope with the formidable fences. These are the 2m. 6f. Topham (formerly John Hughes) Chase and the 2m. 5f. 110yd. Fox Hunters Chase, both part of the National three-day meeting; and the Grand Sefton (2m. 5f. 110yd.) and the Tote Becher Chase (3m. 3f.) held in November.

Bindaree finished fourth in the 2001 John Hughes one year before winning the National. *Monty's Pass* was runner-up in the 2002 Topham Trophy before his National success the following year. However, of these four Aintree races, the longer distance Becher Chase has proved the most informative, the outstanding example being provided by *Amberleigh House*. He had won the 2001 Becher Chase at 33-1, had been runner-up in 2002, and again in 2003 when he was a short head second to *Clan Royal*, who that year also won the Topham. *Amberleigh House* went on to win the 2004 National by three lengths from *Clan Royal*.

As a guide to stamina it is natural to consider form in the major non-Aintree Nationals – the Welsh, Irish, Scottish and Midlands. Seven of the last ten winners at Aintree had won or been placed in one of these. Of the four races the greatest stamina test is the Midlands marathon, run over four and a quarter miles at Uttoxeter. But in general, this race – being held in March, so soon before the Aintree Grand National – has not been an especially useful guide to form in the big one.

To be sure, *Lord Gyllene* finished seven lengths runner-up when carrying 11st. 10lb. in the 1997 Midlands and twenty-three days later, under a mere 10st., romped home by 25 lengths at Aintree. Notably, too, the mare *Laura's Beau* won the Midlands in 1992 and three weeks later finished third at Liverpool. But the fact remains that the last Midlands winner to go on to Aintree glory was *Rag Trade*, successful at Liverpool a year after his 1975 victory at Uttoxeter.

In 1999, *Young Kenny* was the Midlands winner, with *Call It A Day* the runner-up. At Aintree the following year the former was burdened with a 12st. topweight and fell at the tenth and the latter finished sixth. In 2003, six year old *Jurancon II* was third-placed in the Midlands and went on to Aintree as one of four co-favourites. But he fell under champion Tony McCoy at the fourth. One year later *Akarus*, second in the 2003 Midlands, fell at Aintree's sixth fence while *The Bunny Boiler*, the Midlands winner of 2002, finished a distant tenth.

The next longest of these lesser Nationals is the Scottish marathon which, since 1966, has been run at Ayr every April (after the Aintree National) over 4 miles 1 furlong. Like Aintree the course is left-handed and a true stamina test, but unlike Aintree it does not demand great jumping ability.

In 1922, when it was staged at Bogside, *Music Hall* became the first Scottish winner to go on – two years later – to victory at Aintree, a feat immediately emulated by *Sergeant Murphy* in 1923. In reverse *Kellsboro' Jack* won at Bogside in 1935, two years after winning at Aintree. In modern times three Scottish winners – *Merryman II* (1959), *Little Polveir* (1987) and *Earth Summit* (1996)

– achieved Grand National victory one or two years later. But only the great *Red Rum* has pulled off the double in the same year.

Such famed National winners as *Aldaniti*, *Corbiere*, *West Tip* and *Rubstic* (twice runner-up) have suffered defeat at Ayr. The unluckiest was *Freddie* – beaten half a length in the 1964 Scottish National and by three-quarters of a length in the 1965 Aintree National.

Since 1949 the Welsh National has been run at Chepstow over three miles five-and-a-half furlongs. In February 1976, *Rag Trade* became the first winner to go on to glory at Aintree, beating *Red Rum* by two lengths. But since 1979 the Welsh National has been held at the end of December, often with soft or heavy going. In the ensuing years only two winners have also scored at Aintree – *Corbiere* (1982–83) and *Earth Summit* (1997–98).

However, a number of horses have run respectably in the big Chepstow feature before going on to success in the Grand National – *West Tip*, *Rhyme 'N' Reason*, *Party Politics* and *Bindaree*. And the brilliant *Hedgehunter* ran in both Nationals in the season before his Aintree triumph.

Overall, provided they do not encounter entirely different going, horses placed in the Welsh National have a reasonable record in the big one. In 2001, for example, the finishing order at Chepstow was *Supreme Glory*, last year's winner *Jocks Cross*, *Bindaree* and *What's Up Boys*. Three months later *Bindaree* and *What's Up Boys* were first and second respectively in the Grand National. *Supreme Glory* went to Aintree the following year and finished runner-up at 40-1, with *Gunner Welburn*, third at Chepstow in 2002, in fourth place.

In 2003, *Bindaree* returned to Chepstow to win from *Sir Rembrandt* and *Hedgehunter.* At Aintree, as one of four co-favourites, he unseated his rider at the first Becher's. However, *Hedgehunter*, another co-favourite, was a long-time leader, jumping brilliantly until falling at the last. And he would win as 7-1 favourite the following year.

Like the Scottish, the Irish National comes directly after the Aintree race. Run over 3m. 5f. at Fairyhouse, it was first staged in 1870, and in all the years since then only four winners have been successful at Liverpool – *Ascetic Silver* (Irish 1904; Aintree 1906); *Rhyme 'N' Reason* (1985/1988); *Bobbyjo* (1998/1999); and *Numbersixvalverde* (2005/2006). *Papillon*, a close second at Fairyhouse in 1998, won at Aintree in 2000. *Red Marauder* was a distant tenth at Fairyhouse in 2000 before winning at Aintree the following year.

Irish winners who have subsequently failed at Aintree in recent years are: *Omerta* (1991), *Ebony Jane* (1993), *Son of War* (1994), *Feathered Gale* (1996), *Mudahim* (1997), *Davids Lad* (2001) and *The Bunny Boiler* (2002). Of these, only *Ebony Lad* (fourth in 1994, twelfth in 1995) and *The Bunny Boiler* (tenth in 2004) completed the Aintree course. Nevertheless, as previously noted, current trends demand that Irish contenders are regarded with special respect.

Conclusion: *Performances in the above races – especially the Hennessy, the Becher Chase and the Welsh and Irish Nationals – may be taken into consideration at the final stage of elimination, with a look-out for any horse that – as with Lord Gyllene – can be seen to be thrown in at the Grand National weights.*

Chapter 22

STARTING PRICES

THE SHORTEST starting price for a Grand National runner is the 2-1 for the great *Golden Miller* in 1935. He unseated his rider at the 11th. Next shortest is the 5-2 for *Lottery* (pulled up in 1841), *Regal* who finished sixth (remounted) in 1879, and 12-year-old *Conjuror II*, knocked over in 1924.

The shortest price winner is *Poethlyn* who, one year after his success in the 1918 wartime substitute National at Gatwick, went off at 11-4 despite a top weight of 12st. 7lb. The following year, under the same weight, he was a faller at 3-1.

Fortunately, in modern times, no horse has been sent off shorter than the 7-2 for *Red Rum*, when runner-up in 1975. If such a niggardly price ever arose again, the hot favourite would have to be eliminated from the reckoning on the grounds that it was too short to be a betting proposition. By the same token, horses may also be ruled out because their price is too long.

While much play has been made about the "glorious uncertainty" of the Grand National, the fact remains that only four times in the entire history of the race has there been a 100-1 winner. Moreover, three of these four results occurred in circumstances that cannot be duplicated.

The catastrophic pile-up which resulted in no-hoper *Tipperary Tim* winning in 1928 cannot be duplicated because the treacherous ditch at the Canal Turn has since been filled in. The long-priced wins of *Gregalach* (1929) and *Caughoo* (1947) came when the National had its two largest fields, 66 and 57 runners respectively. Since 1984 the field has been restricted to a maximum of 40. Furthermore chances of mass fallers have been reduced by the course modifications of 1990.

To be sure, it may be argued that the National can still be turned into a fiasco by the unpredictable behaviour of a riderless horse, as happened in 1967 when *Foinavon* was the 100-1 winner. But this possibility, too, is much more remote because of the overall improvement in the quality of horses and riders brought about by tighter rules of entry; also because the entry of high quality steeplechasers has been encouraged by changes made to lessen the hazards of certain jumps.

No doubt romantics will continue to insist that a 100-1 winner is always possible. They can argue that bare statistics do not tell the full story: that there could have been six rather than four 100-1 winners if Lord Mildmay on *Davy Jones*, in 1936, had not been deprived of his reins at the penultimate fence, and if Eddie Reavey, with one fence to jump on *Zahia* in 1948, had not incredibly mistaken the proper course ahead.

For further encouragement they can cite the fact that two rank outsiders priced at 200-1 – *Magpie* (1886) and *Melleray's Belle* (1929) – have finished fourth, while no fewer than fifteen 100-1 shots have been placed, five of them as runner-up, and so hugely rewarding each-way punters.

Then again, in the 1999 National, a 200-1 shock was briefly threatened when *Merry People*, almost tailed off after the first circuit, made remarkable progress and emerged to dispute the lead approaching the penultimate fence. Alas, for the first time in his life, the 11-year-old Irish hope was now a faller, being remounted to finish a distant 16th.

The fact is that there will always be punters who dream of miracles. Being aware of this, the bookies began to raise prices to untold heights in the 1980s. In 1983 the field of 41 runners included three 200-1 chances, two priced at 300-1 and, most sensationally, two priced at 500-1. Not one of these long-shots completed the course.

In 1986 the bookies had three runners priced at 500-1; and the following year no fewer than 17 of 40 starters stood at 100-1 or more, with these including a record seven in the 500-1 bracket. Such was the layers' good judgement that only four of the 17 completed the course, the best being *Cranlome*, fourteenth at 500-1. And they got even bolder in 1989, pricing fourteen at 100-1 or more, with three of them initially on offer at an incredible 1,000-1 (later cut to 300-1). Only two of the fourteen completed the course – the best, in eleventh place, being *The Thirsty Farmer*, a Martin Pipe runner available at 200-1.

It illustrates all too clearly that the layers are no fools; and nowadays they have a still greater wealth of information to guide them. Meanwhile, for all those might-have-been stories, the lack of a 100-1 winner since 1967 remains a most daunting statistic. As for 66-1 winners, there have been only three: *Rubio* (1908), *Russian Hero* (1949) and *Ayala* (1963). Four have triumphed at 50-1: *Fobra* (1932), *Sheila's Cottage* (1948), *Anglo* (1968) and *Last Suspect* (1985).

Thus, no winner has been returned at more than 50-1 since 1967, and during the 1990s only one of nine winners (*Royal Athlete*, 40-1) started longer than 16-1.

Since then there have been two winners longer than 16-1: *Red Marauder*, 33-1 in 2001 when only four (two remounted) finished, and *Bindaree*, 20-1 the following year. But statistically, the great majority of winners in the past quarter of a century have come from the range of 15-2 to 16-1.

Conclusion: *In the circumstances I choose to eliminate any horse priced at 50-1 or more. No horse shorter than 9-2 is to be considered as an each-way proposition, though there may be a case for making it the subject of a to-win "cover bet".*

Chapter 23

TIPSTERS

AS ALREADY itemised in the introduction, journalist-tipsters have had some spectacular success in finding Grand National winners; and of them all, none is more influential and worthy of respect than the *Racing Post's Pricewise*. Equally, however, tipsters can get their forecasts spectacularly wrong.

The worst Grand National tips? Before the 1967 *Foinavon* fiasco, racing pundit Charles Benson advised that 100-1 shots "can be safely ignored, even in a race noted for shocks". An excusable error in the circumstances. Then again, on the TV *Morning Line* of National Day, 1996, John Francome proclaimed: "You can scrub him (*Rough Quest*) out. He has not got his ground. He has had a hard race at Cheltenham. He has fallen twice this year and he would need to travel in a horse-box to get the trip".

But perhaps the prize for the biggest misjudgement should go to Mark Winstanley who in 1997, one year before the sad demise of *The Sporting Life*, wrote that *Lord Gyllene* "has as much chance of success as Ginger Spice joining a convent. This slowcoach has not got the class to win a National and I will be amazed if he reaches a place." And for good measure he said of *Camelot Knight*, "there is more chance of Anneka Rice finding the Holy Grail than this horse has of finishing in the first dozen."

Lord Gyllene led from start to finish to win by 25

lengths. *Camelot Knight* came home third at 100-1. At least, to his credit, this popular tipster's selection, *Suny Bay*, did finish second; and in 1998 he did tip the fourth placed *St Mellion Fairway* before the horse was cut from 40-1 to 20-1.

While ex-jockeys such as Peter Scudamore and Francome have sometimes displayed inspired judgement in their forecasts, the record shows that for the most part current jockeys deserve their reputation for being notoriously bad tipsters. As for telephone tipsters, who charge for their recommendations, one can only agree with John McCririck who has observed: "If the pedlars of tips have any real value, why are they in business? Why aren't they making a killing following their own advice?"

I concur with that view while hastening to reiterate that the system recommended here is not designed for speculators seeking to "make a killing" but for the modest punter hoping to have a good run for a modest outlay.

For a far-ranging view of tipsters' selections, one may choose on Grand National Day to consult the *Racing Post's* Naps Competition Table featuring the first choices of some 55 newspaper tipsters. Here many of the tipsters, though not all, will nap a horse in the National. But analysis of their more recent naps is not especially encouraging.

In 1999 eleven National runners were napped, the most popular selections being *Fiddling The Facts* (five naps) and *Eudipe* (four), both of whom were fallers at the second Becher's. *Bobbyjo*, the winner, had two naps. In 2000 the most napped runner, *Star Traveller* (four) was pulled up at the 27th, the race being won by *Papillon*, one of three horses with three naps each and, valuably, the most favoured choice of newspaper correspondents polled in an eve-of-the-National BBC TV preview.

In 2001 the most napped were *Beau* (six) and *Edmond* (five). The former fell at the 20th, the latter at the 15th. In 2002, more usefully, the winner *Bindaree* was the second most napped horse with five votes to the nine of *Beau* (unseated rider at the 14th). In 2003, nine runners were napped and far and away the favourite was *Chives* (pulled up at the 12th) with seven naps. In 2004 seven horses were napped, headed by *Clan Royal* (runner-up) and *Josh Naylor* (pulled up before the 19th). In 2005 non-finishers *Take The Stand* and *Strong Resolve* led with seven and five naps respectively. Winner *Hedgehunter* had four.

The 2006 National was seen as being so open that no fewer than 14 different horses were napped – headed by *Hedgehunter* and *Ross Comm* (four each), and *Garvivonnian* and *Jack High* (three). Only two correspondents napped the winner, *Numbersixvalverde.*

Conclusion: *Overall, as indicated by the naps table record, tips in themselves are of limited value. At the same time, the long-term record of Pricewise demands that his selection should be given special consideration and not dismissed lightly. Otherwise, for our purposes, tips are only useful to some degree where the tipster presents solid reasoning behind his selection and perhaps pinpoints some overlooked information about a horse's preparation, best distance and favoured going.*

Chapter 24

TRAINERS

SINCE WORLD WAR II only six champion trainers have saddled the Grand National winner – Fred Rimell (four times), Neville Crump and Vincent O'Brien (three), Fred Winter (two) and Fulke Walwyn and Martin Pipe (one). Those who have been denied success at Aintree include Ryan Price (five times the title-holder), Peter Cazalet, Michael Dickinson and Mick Easterby (all three times champion trainer) and Nicky Henderson and David Nicholson (twice leading trainer).

Remarkably, Pipe, 15 times champion, has had more Grand National runners than any other trainer in history, and yet he has produced only one winner, *Miinnehoma*. In 2001 he was unsuccessful despite having a record ten runners – a quarter of the field. By 2006 he had had 57 non-finishers out of 81 starters with 35 failing to complete the first circuit. Similarly, his greatest rival and new champion trainer Paul Nicholls has had 33 runners with only one (2005 runner-up *Royal Auclair*) making the frame.

Thus, it may be seen that a high strike-rate in National Hunt racing does not necessarily point to success in the Grand National. More significant is a record that shows consistent adeptness at turning out long-distance chasers of high quality – an outstanding example in modern times being Jenny Pitman who saddled two winners, one second and three thirds at Aintree, and over the years won all the other major Nationals – Welsh, Scottish and Irish.

Conclusion: *Grand National contenders are not to be favoured simply because they are sent out by highly successful trainers. For the purpose of considering selections the great value of trainers derives from the comments they make about their National entries. This is the closest the ordinary punter comes to gaining inside information; and in the build-up to the National all interviews with trainers should be carefully scanned for vital facts about their Aintree entries.* See, Chapter 27: The System In Action.

Chapter 25

WEIGHTS

SINCE 1937 the minimum weight to be carried in the National has been fixed at 10st. In the 1960s no fewer than four horses won off the lowest mark. But in the 1970s only one (*Rubstic*, 1979) was successful, and since then only three runners set to carry the minimum have won the race – *Little Polveir* (1989, carrying 3lb. overweight), *Lord Gyllene* (1997) and *Bobbyjo* (1999).

More significantly, no horse has carried top weight to victory in Aintree's showpiece since 1977 when *Red Rum* defied 11st. 8lb. to romp home by 25 lengths for his third National success; and since the 1983 win of *Corbiere* on 11st. 4lb., only two winners (*Rhyme 'N' Reason*, 1988, and *Hedgehunter*, 2005) have carried as much as 11st. to victory. However, in 1998, *Suny Bay*, top-weighted with 12st., did magnificently well to finish runner-up to *Earth Summit* (receiving 23lb.) and, most unusually, in 2002, runner-up *What's Up Boys* and fourth placed *Kingsmark* were both carrying more than 11st. 5lb.

Curiously, following the success of *Emblem* in 1863, more than 140 years passed without a horse carrying 10st. 10lb. to victory in the National. But that odd statistic finally ended in 2004 when a late 3lb. rise in the weights saw *Amberleigh House* triumph on that elusive mark.

Overall, statistics of recent decades weigh in favour of the winner coming more often than not from within the range of 10st. 3lb. to 10st. 12lb. Such contenders in the handicap proper are not to be lightly dismissed.

In 1985, for example, *The Times* A-Z guide said, "*Last Suspect* can be safely crossed off your list". Yet the gelding, on 10st. 5lb., had never fallen in a race and was a sound jumper and a dour stayer. He won at 50-1. Similarly, in 1995, Jenny Pitman's *Royal Athlete* was on 10st. 6lb. when he won at 40-1.

On the other hand, there was a suggestion in 2005 that horses burdened with 11st.-plus might begin to make an impression more often as a result of the handicapper's endeavours to raise the quality of entries by giving top-class chasers a rather more generous weight than they might receive in other handicap races.

That year, for the first time, all 40 starters were in the "handicap proper", carrying 10st. 5lb. or more; and the result was a win for *Hedgehunter* on 11st. 1lb. with the 14 lengths runner-up, *Royal Auclair*, carrying a massive 11st. 10lb.

On the eve of the 2006 Grand National, John Francome was still boldly advising punters to "stick with the horses below 11st. in the handicap." But this policy was now looking decidedly dodgy with all horses again in the "handicap proper", and with such a high-class chaser as *Hedgehunter*, impressive runner-up in the Cheltenham Gold Cup, challenging on a top weight (shared with *Royal Auclair*) of 11st. 12lb. As it happened, *Hedgehunter*, 5-1 joint favourite, finished six lengths runner-up.

Conclusion: *Though recognising the risk, for the time being I choose to continue eliminating all horses carrying 11st. 5lb. or more. If, after following the first two stages of elimination, more than six runners still remain, then rule out any horse carrying over 11st. 1lb.*

Chapter 26

THE ELIMINATION SYSTEM EXPLAINED

THE MOST eccentric punter I know is a 70-year-old betting shop habitué who, several times a year, excitedly tells me that he has discovered a new winning system. One time his system might simplistically involve backing the two top-weighted horses in conditions races; another time it could be betting on horses coming out within a week of their last appearance.

All it means is that, by monitoring results daily, he has observed a succession of similar results that are entirely coincidental. Inevitably, this pattern soon comes to an end and, after suffering too many reversals, he goes back to the drawing-board to resume his relentless search for a winning formula.

If he must bet on such a basis, I tell him, he might be better occupied just following the selections of the *Racing Post's Pricewise* who, over the years, has produced some sensational winning runs. But stubbornly he continues to go his own futile way in seeking the Punter's Holy Grail.

Quite simply, there is no foolproof, hard-and-fast system; and all winning patterns must sooner or later come to an end. The Elimination System is only different in that its procedures are not written in stone but are always subject to revision to allow for changing conditions and emerging trends.

For example, as explained in the handicapping

section, a key factor in our success in the 1980s and 1990s was the feasibility of eliminating all horses not in the "handicap proper." This was never more advantageous than in 1990 and 1995 when there were only eleven horses carrying more than the 10st. minimum, greatly aiding a final six-horse selection for each-way backing that took in the winners *Mr Frisk* (16-1) and *Royal Athlete* (40-1) respectively, plus runners-up *Durham Edition* (9-1) and *Dubacilla* (16-1) and fourth-placed *Party Politics* (9-1) and *Brown Windsor* (7-1).

However, there was now growing evidence that the automatic elimination of out-of-the-handicap horses was becoming a risky proposition, The final proof came in 1999 when, following the appointment of a new senior handicapper with new objectives, long-handicap horses (*Bobbyjo* and *Blue Charm*) finished first and second respectively. Clearly, after that rare losing year, it was necessary for the system to be revised, with out-of-the-handicap horses only being eliminated as a last resort.

Fortunately, by this time, a new trend had emerged to aid the elimination process: the fact that no horse had carried more than 11st. to victory since *Corbiere* won in 1983 on 11st. 4lb. This sequence would not be interrupted until 2005 when *Hedgehunter* won under a burden just one pound over the 11st. mark, with *Royal Auclair* ominously taking second place under 11st. 10lb.

In the same way, the easing of Aintree's most formidable fences in 1990 had also led to changes in the system. Subsequently, there were increasing signs that the character of the race was changing, with less emphasis on clean jumping ability and more on galloping pace and power. As a result, I no longer discriminated against horses with an F in their seasonal results: a most rewarding change as it proved in 2001 when the National was won by *Red Marauder*, a 33-1 shot who had fallen in his last race and who was to be described by his jockey-trainer Richard Guest as "probably the worst jumper ever to win a National".

Further evidence of the greater emphasis on speed came with the successful Irish ploy of tuning up contenders over hurdles.

In 1999 *Bobbyjo* won a two-mile hurdle race immediately prior to his success at Aintree. In 2003 *Monty's Pass* prepared for Aintree with two spins over a mere two miles in novices' hurdles. In 2005 *Hedgehunter* had five hurdle races to protect his handicap mark, tackling fences only after he had secured a favourable weight for the National. And in 2006 *Numbersixvalverde* had two hurdles races before winning at Aintree.

Such preparation now needs to be viewed with suspicion when evaluating form. Meanwhile the objective of the Elimination System remains the same: to reduce the National field to no more than six runners, all of which – presuming none are shorter than 9-2 – will be evenly backed each-way.

Of course, backing so many horses in one race will be anathema to the regular, year-round punter who is likely to be a keen follower of form and inclined to take pride in making his or her own selection for the Grand National. The Elimination System is not designed for such a devotee of National Hunt racing but strictly for the occasional or once-a-year punter with limited or no knowledge of form.

Essentially, the system serves a dual purpose. Firstly,

it is designed to ensure that, however many fallers there may be, the backer is likely to have an interest in a lively contender throughout the race. Secondly, as a consolation, it provides a good chance that any failure to find the winner is likely to be offset by returns on one or more selections running into a place.

Six horses, however, is the absolute maximum to be backed, and five the minimum. Any more or less and the prospects of a sufficient return without the winner are too greatly diminished. Altogether, there are three stages of elimination to be operated after the final declaration of runners, the process being stopped as soon as fewer than seven horses remain.

STAGE ONE

Eliminate:

a) Horses aged under eight or over twelve.

b) Any horse automatically allotted top weight as a result of failure. to qualify for handicapping purposes.

c) Horses carrying 11st. 5lb. or more.

d) All horses generally priced at 50-1 or more on the eve of the National.

e) Any horse making its seasonal debut.

f) All horses positively unsuited by the prevailing "going". [See, Chapter 27: The System In Action].

IF (as is very probable) more than six runners remain, we move on to Stage Two.

STAGE TWO

Eliminate:

a) Unless heavy going prevails, *as far as possible** horses that have never been placed in chases over three miles or more. (*Form guides may only record their places in the past one or two seasons, but all their winning distances are listed).

b) Unless it is "thrown in" on a low weight, any horse that has had a hard race at the preceding Cheltenham Festival.

c) Any previous winner of the Grand National.

d) Any non-Irish horse without previous experience in English chases.

e) Any horse without a prep race after the turn of the year.

f) Any horse acknowledged to have had an interrupted preparation; or, in the event of circumstances (e.g. a big winter freeze-up or foot-and-mouth) has not had the benefit of a recent run.

IF fewer than seven horses remain, stop the process and make those surviving your selections. If not, move on to Stage Three, making eliminations in the designated order and stopping *as soon as* fewer than seven remain.

STAGE THREE

Eliminate:

a) Horses wearing blinkers or a visor.
b) Horses carrying more than 11st. 1lb.
c) Horses running from "out of the handicap".
d) Any horse – excepting a Maryland Hunt Cup winner – that has never won a Listed or Graded (Class 1) chase. (Check with *Racing Post* Form Guide).
e) Any remaining French-bred horse.

IF, as is most unlikely, more than six still remain, make the six with the shortest prices your selections for backing.

IF, at this stage, you should need to choose between

horses tied on the same price, then favour a) any horse that has raced over hurdles to protect its handicap mark; b) a horse that has run well in the Hennessy Gold Cup, the Becher Chase, or the Welsh or Irish Nationals; c) the horse with most wins over three miles or more; d) a horse perceived to be especially well bred.

Once there are fewer than seven selections remaining, they should all be backed evenly each-way, or to-win if shorter than 9-2. It is a method most especially suited for family or friends gathered to watch the National, with it being possible to allot one or two horses to each member of the group.

The stakes? The aim is to enjoy having a runner involved throughout the race and hopefully make a modest profit. The golden rule is that you should never bet a total sum that you cannot lose without reasonable equanimity. Gain without pain is the objective. My own preference is for a maximum of six bets of £5 each-way, making a total stake of £60. More cautious punters may favour just £1 each-way at a total cost of £12, or even 50p each-way with only £6 at risk.

One final point about each-way betting. In all handicap races where there are 16 or more runners – as in the National – bookmakers traditionally pay one-fourth the win odds for the first, second, third and fourth finishers. Thus, in operating this system, I have expected, almost always successfully, that any failure to find the winner will be financially offset by having backed at least one of the other three "placed" horses.

However, it should be noted that a few of the smaller bookmakers – outside the Big Three (William Hill,

Ladbrokes and Coral) – have now begun to be more competitive by offering to pay out on the *fifth* finisher. Obviously, therefore, it can now pay to shop around and take advantage of this more attractive offer.

Chapter 27

THE SYSTEM IN ACTION

THE ELIMINATION System demands a modicum of homework on the part of the punter – most importantly in noting those horses clearly unsuited by the going that prevails on Grand National day.

It can also be useful to keep notes on performances in key chases from October or November onwards. But no matter if this does not appeal to the casual punter. It is entirely acceptable to delay all such work until February, thereafter simply relying on form guides to consider earlier results.

The homework should begin in earnest following the announcement of the allotted National weights in February. From that point on it is helpful to keep a notebook recording any valuable information about likely runners – e.g. trainers' comments on their form, preferred going etc. Better still, if possible, keep the notes on a computer where they can be more easily updated, or deleted in the case of a horse that is withdrawn.

Obviously, the more information gathered the better, and thus habitual punters are likely to be on the look-out for relevant reports in the *Racing Post* every day. But for the one-off National punter this involves a financial burden that can seriously deduct from any gains on the race itself. For our purposes, therefore, one may rely largely on one's daily newspaper; at the same time being sure to get the *Racing Post* on the day after the weights are announced, and *every day* of the week of the Grand

National. In addition, I recommend getting *The Racing Post Weekender* on the Wednesday before the National.

Here then, for guidance, is a diary recording my observations and procedures prior to the running of the 2006 Grand National, with a step-by-step account of eliminations made after the final declaration of runners:

February 2 2006

It is announced that 148 have been nominated for the Grand National, among them nine of the first ten home last year and Gold Cup aspirants *Monkerhostin* and *Ollie Magern*. A record 38 entries are from Ireland and, as usual, Martin Pipe leads trainers with 22 entries. Ladbrokes' betting at this stage is: 8-1 *Clan Royal*, 10-1 *Hedgehunter*, 16-1 *Silver Birch*, *Royal Auclair*, 25-1 *Cornish Rebel, Colnel Rayburn, Ebony Light, Eurotrek, Innox, Jack High, Lord Of Illusion, Numbersixvalverde*, 33-1 others.

February 14

The senior jumps handicapper unveils the weights he has allotted to 144 of 148 entries (four were not qualified). *Monkerhostin* heads the list on 11st. 12lb., followed by *Hedgehunter* and *Royal Auclair*, last year's winner and runner-up on 11st. 10lb. Eighty-five entries are in the handicap proper compared with a record 92 last year and there is every prospect that the entire National field will again be set to run from within the handicap proper.

Even at this stage some horses can be eliminated on grounds of age or weight. But, for the sake of clarification, we will delay beginning the process until we know the final 40-horse line-up, by which time the weights may have been raised.

February 15

Following publication of the weights, *Clan Royal* is naturally all the rage, having been awarded a mere 10st. 8lb. – three pounds more than he carried as runner-up in the 2004 National, but three pounds less than in last year's National when, going strongly six lengths in the lead, he was desperately unlucky to be carried out by a loose horse approaching Becher's second time around.

The *Racing Post* provides a form guide for all the leading contenders; and the many reported comments by trainers (their reaction to the weights and any reference to the going wanted) are duly noted. Tom Segal (*Pricewise*) picks out *Silver Birch* (16-1) and *Numbersixvalverde* (25-1) as value bets. Craig Thake (*Big Race Trends*) names *Clan Royal*, *Silver Birch* and Irish raiders *Another Rum* and *Numbersixvalverde* as the entries that have most appeal.

Last year, at this stage, we profitably had two non-system "fun bets" of £2 to win on the strongly fancied 25-1 shots *Timbera* and *Hedgehunter*. This year a case can clearly be made for similar win bets on *Clan Royal* (8-1), *Silver Birch* and *Numbersixvalverde.* However, we decide – wrongly as it would prove – not to be tempted into betting ante-post.

February 18

Grand National entries make their first appearance in force. A number of leading fancies disappoint, most notably *Silver Birch* who, as 2-1 favourite, is pulled up before the 16th in the Country Gentlemen's Association Chase over three miles one-and-a-half furlongs at Wincanton. The soft going was supposed to suit, but he made a bad mistake at the ninth and was never travelling well. Trainer Paul Nicholls was mystified and as a result

Silver Birch drifted out to 20-1 in the National betting. *Iris Royal* was a far distant last of five finishers.

At Haydock (heavy) nine National entries compete in the Red Square Vodka Gold Cup, formerly the Greenalls Grand National Trial, run over an extended three and a half miles and won in 1977 by *Suny Bay* who went on to be runner-up in the next two Grand Nationals. Only one made any real impression: *Sir Rembrandt* (11st. 5lb.) finishing a well-beaten third when conceding 19lb. to the winner (*Ossmoses*), and far behind in fourth was *Tyneandthyneagain* (10st. 8lb.) followed by *L'Aventure* (11st.).

Distant finishers were *Double Honour* (11st.) and *Ebony Light* (10st. 11lb.). Six-year-old *Joaaci* (11st. 5lb.) was a long way off fourth when he fell absolutely legless at the last. Tailed off and pulled up were 13-year-old *First Gold* (11st.), *Chives* (11st. 6lb.) and *Eurotrek* (11st. 8lb). As a result *Sir Rembrandt*, still aiming for the Cheltenham Gold Cup, was cut from 25-1 to 20-1 in the National betting. The others showed nothing to encourage ante-post backers.

Meanwhile, at Uttoxeter (heavy), four National entries were on parade in the Singer and Friedlander Handicap Chase, now run over two miles six and a half furlongs and no longer a significant Aintree trial. They were *Be My Better Half* (10st. 13lb.), fourth; *Haut de Gamme* (11st. 9lbs), fifth; *Amberleigh House* (11st. 2lb.), a distant seventh; and *Juveigneur* (11st. 11lb.), pulled up before two out and after several mistakes. Of these, *Haut de Gamme* and *Amberleigh House* ran satisfactorily over a distance far too short.

The latter, totally unsuited by the going, went out to 50-1 for the National. Undaunted, Ginger McCain confirmed Graham Lee as his jockey and said: "I know it sounds daft, but these days I think he needs five miles".

At Lingfield, also unsuited by heavy ground, *Fondmort* finished eight lengths third in a chase over two miles four and a half furlongs. A solid performance but all his wins have been over two miles five furlongs or less.

March 17

Carrying the standard 11st. 10lb., *Hedgehunter* is hugely impressive in finishing second to *War of Attrition* in the Cheltenham Gold Cup – so much so that Ladbrokes cut him from 10-1 to 4-1 favouritism for the Grand National. Thus, the Elimination System will be most sorely tested since *Hedgehunter* already qualifies for elimination with a weight over 11st. 5lb. and as a former National winner. But the fact remains that *Rough Quest*, the 1996 Gold Cup runner-up, is the only horse since 1934 to win at Aintree after being placed in the Gold Cup, and he had a huge advantage in being lightly weighted at Aintree on 10st. 7lb. and facing only 26 opponents. On the other hand, *Hedgehunter* has three weeks to recover from his Gold Cup exertions whereas *Rough Quest* had only two.

Among winners at Cheltenham is National entry *Fondmort* (11st.), but only in a Grade 2 chase over his favoured distance of 2m. 5f.

March 18

The Midlands Grand National Handicap Chase over 4m. 1f. 110yd. is held at Uttoxeter (heavy) and won by *GVA Ireland* (10st. 3lb.) with Ruby Walsh, by four lengths from *Ossmoses* (11st. 5lb.), then 14 lengths back *to L'Aventure* (11st. 2lb.) and six lengths to *Victory*

Gunner (10st. 2lb.). Aintree National entries pulled up are *Control Man* (10st. 11lb), *Marcus Du Berlais* (11st. 1lb.), *Baron Windrush* (11st. 6lb.), and *Philson Run* (11st. 5lb.).

March 21

Following the defection of *Monkerhostin* at the second forfeit stage, the weights automatically rise 2lb. so that *Hedgehunter* and *Royal Auclair* will now have to carry the top weight of 11st. 12lb. The last horse to carry a similar weight to victory was *Red Rum* with 12st. in 1974. *Hedgehunter* carried 11st 1lb. when beating *Royal Auclair* (11st. 10lb.) by 14 lengths in last year's National. At this stage 96 entries remain – 58 of them in the handicap proper.

April 1

The Grand National prices are absurdly tight with *Hedgehunter* as short as 4-1 with Ladbrokes and no longer than 11-2; *Clan Royal*, 6-1 best with Ladbrokes; *Numbersixvalverde* 12-1 and *Innox* 14-1. As McCoy rightly observes in the *Daily Telegraph*: "4-1 or 5-1 in a 40-runner handicap is ridiculous and if the bookmakers had any bottle it would be 9-1 the field in the National". If such skinny odds remain it will be difficult to make a sizeable profit backing six horses each-way in a year when the market leaders have strong claims in a class field likely to have all runners in the handicap proper. *Hedgehunter* – to be eliminated according to the System – holds the key. He will need to be another *Red Rum* if he is to win back-to-back Nationals after an excellent but hard run in the Cheltenham Gold Cup. He has the outstanding help of Ruby Walsh but, as trainer Willie Mullins says, "Statistics and history would be against him."

April 3

Eighty-four entries, headed by *Hedgehunter*, remain at the five-day stage. Horses on 10st. 5lb. are in danger of missing the cut and clearly all 40 will again run from within the handicap proper. Marcus Armytage observes in the *Daily Telegraph* that the race has effectively become a limited handicap and "we are bound to get more horses carrying more than 11st winning". The going – at present good to soft with some soft patches – is crucial. More rain is very possible and as Armytage writes: "On soft ground each pound over 11st. will feel like a stone".

April 4

The Racing Post Weekender provides a valuable guide to all the runners. Tipsters' selections – Mark Winstanley: *Numbersixvalverde*, *Jack High* and long-shot *Le Duc*; Mel Cullinan: *Hedgehunter* and *Haut de Gamme*. Nick Mordin, Systems Analyst, reduces the field by elimination to seven: *Garvivonnian*, *Heros Collonges*, *Jack High*, *Clan Royal*, *Lord Atterbury*, *Nil Desperandum* and *Numbersixvalverde*, and suggests a perm of the four Irish-trained runners – *Garvivonnian*, *Jack High*, *Nil Desperandum* and *Numbersixvalverde* – in computer straight forecasts since the Irish have gone 1-2 in three of the last four big British jump races. Malcolm Heyhoe picks out *Numbersixvalverde* and names *Juveigneur* as the best outsider. Dick Hunter goes for *Garvivonnian*, followed by *Clan Royal*, *Hedgehunter* and long-shot *Lord Atterbury*. Alistair Whitehouse-Jones picks *Clan Royal*, with *Numbersixvalverde* as the best alternative. Dave Edwards suggests *Innox*.

April 7

The eve of the Grand National and the 40-runner line-up is finally resolved as:

Royal Auclair (22) Fr P. Nicholls 9.11.12. C. Williams
Hedgehunter (22) Ire W.P. Mullins. 10.11.12.
R. Walsh
Cornish Rebel (22) Ire P. Nicholls 9.11.9. J. Tizzard
Therealbandit (103) Ire M. Pipe 9.11.9. R. Johnson
It Takes Time (49) Ire M.Pipe 12.11.8 T.J. Murphy
Le Roi Miguel (23) Fr P. Nicholls 8.11.7 L. Heard
Native Upmanship (55) Ire A. Moore 13.11.0
C. O'Dwyer
Innox (42) Fr F. Doumen. 10.10.13 R. Thornton
Silver Birch (42) Ire P.Nicholls 9.10.12 S. Thomas
Whispered Secret (23) Ger M.Pipe. 7.10.12 R.Greene
Rincẹ Ri (42) Ire T.Walsh 13.10.12 A.J.McNamara
Puntal (484) Fr M.Pipe 10.10.12 B.J. Geraghty
Lord Of Illusion (22) Ire T. George 9.10.11
J.M. Maguire
Ebony Light (49) Ire D.McCain 10.10.10 S.J.Craine
First Gold (49) Fr F.Doumen. 13.10.10 R. McGrath
Clan Royal (27) Fr Jonjo O'Neill 11.10.0
A.P. McCoy
Le Duc (97) Fr P. Nicholls 7.10.10 J .E.Moore
Sir OJ (23) Ire N. Meade 9.10.10 P.Carberry
Forest Gunner (103) R.Ford 12.10.10
Miss N. Carberry
Joes Edge (22) Ire F. Murphy 9.10.10 D.N. Russell
Juveigneur (25) Fr N. Henderson 9.10.9
M.A. Fitzgerald
Amberleigh House (19) Ire D. McCain 14.10.9
G. Lee
Ballycassidy (22) Ire P. Bowen 10.10.9 L. Aspell

Inca Trail (29) Ire D. McCain 10.10.9 B. Harding
Garvivonnian (42) Ire E. Mitchell 11.10.8 G. Cotter
Numbersixvalverde (27) Ire M. Brassil 10.10.8
N.P. Madden
Iznogoud (22) Fr M. Pipe 10.10.8 T. Scudamore
Jack High (22) Ire T. Walsh 11.10.7 D.J. Casey
Haut De Gamme (49) Fr F. Murphy 11.10.7 K. Mercer
Nil Desperandum (22) Ire M. Crowley 9.10.7
T.P. Treacy
Baron Windrush (21) N. Twiston-Davies 11.10.7
C. Llewellyn
Heros Collognes (32) Fr P. Nicholls 11.10.7
J.P. McNamara
Tyneandthyneagain (49) J Howard Johnson 11.10.7
P. Buchanan
Risk Accessor (24) Ire Jonjo O'Neill 11.10.6 N. Fehily
Direct Access (133) Ire N. Richards 11.10.6
A. Dobbin
Colnel Rayburn (41) Ire P. Nolan 10.10.6 J. Cullen
Iris Royal (49) Fr N. Henderson 10.10.6 M. Foley
Ross Comm (14) Mrs S.J. Smith 10.10.5 D. Elsworth
Shotgun Willy (385) Ire R.C. Guest 12.10.5
A. Tinkler
Just In Debt (25) Ire M. Todhunter 10.10.4
A. Dempsey

The elimination process can now begin.

STAGE ONE

(a) we discard the runners under eight years old and over 12 years old. Therefore, out go: *Native Upmanship, Whispered Secret, Rince Ri, First Gold, Le Duc* and *Amberleigh House.* Thirty-four remain.

b) We eliminate all horses carrying more than 11st. 5lb.

– a big gamble since this year it takes in an exceptional class horse in *Hedgehunter*, who won by a comfortable 14 lengths last year and most recently ran a blinder as runner-up in the Cheltenham Gold Cup. However, all the statistics are against him as a past winner carrying top weight three weeks after a hard race at Cheltenham. He would need to be another *Red Rum* to win back-to-back Nationals under a top weight of 11st. 12lb. Yet this is not impossible; and he has the benefit of the jockey with the best record of current riders in Nationals: Ruby Walsh.

Nevertheless, we must stick to the system until it fails, and so we now lose *Hedgehunter*, last year's runner-up *Royal Auclair*, *Cornish Rebel*, *Therealbandit*, *It Takes Time* and *Le Roi Miguel*. Thus, the 40-strong field has been reduced to 28.

c) Requires elimination of any horse automatically allotted top weight as a result of failure to qualify for handicapping purposes. No candidates.

d) We eliminate all horses generally priced at 50-1 or more. Thus we lose: *Ebony Light*, *Forest Gunner*, *Ballycassidy*, *Baron Windrush*, *Heros Collognes*, *Iznogoud*, *Just In Debt*, *Risk Accessor*, *Puntal*, *Iris Royal*, *Shotgun Willy*, and *Tyneandthyneagain*. Sixteen runners remain.

e) Requires elimination of any horse making its seasonal debut. *Puntal*, appearing for the first time in 484 days, has already been deleted.

f) The elimination of any horse unsuited by the going. At present this next *most important* step cannot be taken since the state of the going on Grand National day remains uncertain.

April 8

Grand National Day

7.a.m. We collect the *Racing Post*, allowing plenty of time to study the latest reports from stables with special regard to references to the favoured going of horses. The race is seen as being so open that 14 different runners are napped.

Hedgehunter and *Ross Comm* have the most naps (four), followed by *Jack High* and *Garvivonnian* (three). The respected tipster Gerald Delamere selects *Numbersixvalverde* to win. But interestingly *Pricewise* writes that he has "sort of gone off him (his ante-post selection), having studied his jumping techniques closely, but he is probably the strongest stayer in the field and if he gets into a rhythm and is still there on the second circuit, he will have a good chance".

8.a.m. We watch Channel 4's *Morning Line*, paying special attention to news of the state of the ground at Aintree, with a view to eliminating horses unsuited by the prevailing going. Following overnight rain the course is good to soft with good in patches. There is the possibility of more showers later in the day and, with prices shortening, we take a chance on eliminating horses said to prefer good going: *Joes Edge*, *Juveigneur*, *Lord Of Illusion*, *Nil Desperandum*, *Silver Birch* and *Jack High*. Ten remain.

With Stage One completed we move on to
STAGE TWO, beginning with

a) horses who only have form over less than three miles. Just one qualifies for elimination: *Sir OJ*. Nine remain.

b) Unless it is "thrown in" at a low weight, eliminate

any horse that has had a hard race at the preceding Cheltenham Festival. Only *Hedgehunter* (already eliminated) qualifies.

c) Eliminate any previous winner of the Grand National. Again only *Hedgehunter* qualifies.

d) Eliminate any non-Irish horse without previous experience in English chases. None qualify.

e) Eliminate any horse without a prep race after the turn of the year. These are *Therealbandit* and *Forest Gunner* (already eliminated) and *Roselier*-sired *Direct Access*. Eight remain.

f) Eliminate any horse that has had an interrupted preparation. We dispense with *Colnel Rayburn* since connections say that his preparation has not been as good as last year when, after several jumping mistakes in the National, he was pulled up before the 27th. Seven remain.

The remaining seven are: *Clan Royal*, *Garvivonnian*, *Numbersixvalverde*, *Innox*, *Haut De Gamme*, *Inca Trail* and *Ross Comm*. One too many.

STAGE THREE

a) Eliminate any horse wearing blinkers. These are *Sir OJ* and *First Gold* (already out), *Innox* and *Inca Trail.* We cannot discriminate between the two qualifiers and so we eliminate both, leaving just five runners rather than the minimum six required. Those to be backed each-way are *Clan Royal*, *Garvivonnian*, *Numbersixvalverde*, *Haut de Gamme* and *Ross Comm.*

If it had been necessary to complete Stage Three, the only further casualties would have been *Clan Royal* and *Haut de Gamme*, qualifying for last resort elimination as French-bred runners.

10.a.m. The phone rings. As usual a handful of friends and relatives – once-a-year punters – are beginning to call. As usual, they seek my opinion and, being strangers to betting shops, want me to place a bet on their behalf. I give them my five selections; and, as usual, every one stubbornly or proudly chooses to back only a single runner. It is the way of the world; the same impulse that drives the hit-or-miss dreamer to buy a national lottery ticket or place a chip on a single number at roulette. Only one of them enjoys having made a successful choice.

4.20 p.m. After a false start, we watch the race unfold on television, growing ever more nervous as the eliminated *Hedgehunter* runs magnificently under our favourite jump jockey, Ruby Walsh. He is left in the lead at Valentines second time around. But ultimately the weight and going count against him and he is outpaced by six lengths on the run-in. The result of our five backed £5 each-way is as follows:
Clan Royal (11-2 at time of bet) 3rd won £1.87
Garvivonnian (14-1) pulled up after 16th lost £10.00
Numbersixvalverde (11-1) won £68.75
Ross Comm (16-1) fell 4th lost £10.00
Haut De Gamme (25-1) fell 20th lost £10.00

Happily this was a most satisfactory outcome: a gain of £40.62 and importantly the pleasure of having runners in contention throughout. On the other hand, we do recognise that it was a close-run thing in what was an exceptionally difficult year.

Charles Barnett, Aintree's managing director, fairly described the 2006 race as "the best Grand National ever in terms of quality". For the second successive year, Phil Smith had succeeded in attracting such high-class chasers that all 40 contenders were running in the handicap proper and all were at least four pounds above the 10st. minimum.

Admittedly, in operating the System, we had one major stroke of good fortune. It may be argued that, but for the overnight rain preceding the Grand National, *Hedgehunter* (qualified for elimination whatever the "going") would have emulated *Red Rum's* back-to-back wins. He is a truly outstanding chaser. And as long as Mr Smith continues to attract such quality and so effectively compress the weights, there remains a real danger of a horse carrying more than 11st. 5lb. to victory.

Interestingly, this National had twelve French-bred runners and only one (*Clan Royal*) completed the course. Bearing in mind that a French-bred horse has not won the National since *Lutteur III* in 1909, there is encouragement for eliminating all such runners.

To be sure, the French-bred *Puntal* did well to finish sixth when having his first outing for 484 days, but he was a distance and 16 lengths off the winner. So we will continue to eliminate horses making their seasonal debut. Also, despite *Hedgehunter's* heroic effort, we will make no adjustment to the current system.

Other books from SportsBooks

Growing up with Subbuteo
Mark Adolph
The story of the man who invented Subbuteo by his son.
Paperback. ISBN 1899807 40 3 £7.99

Accrington Stanley - the club that wouldn't die
Phil Whalley
Accrington Stanley returned to the Football League this year after resigning in 1962. This tells the story of the years of struggle and eventual triumph.
Hardback. ISBN 1899807 47 0 £16.99

Fitba Gallimaufry
Adam Scott
Everything you need to know about Scottish football and some things you don't.
Hardback ISBN 1899807 45 4 £9.99

All-Time Greats of British Athletics
Mel Watman
Profiles of the greatest British athletes from Walter George to Paula Radcliffe.
Paperback ISBN 1899807 44 6 4 £15.00

Ode to Jol
Alasdair Gold
A sideways, and very funny, look at Tottenham Hotspur's' 2005/06 season.
Paperback. ISBN 1899807 43 8 £12.99

Wembley – The Complete Record 1923–2000
Glen Isherwood
Every football match ever played at the world's most iconic football stadium is detailed in this exhaustive reference work.
Paperback. ISBN 1899807 42 X £14.99

Harry Potts – Margaret's Story
Margaret Potts and Dave Thomas
Harry Potts was Burnley's manager in the days the small-town team won the league and reached the FA Cup final. Great photographic section.
Hardback. ISBN 1899807 41 1 £17.99

Ha'Way/Howay the Lads
Alan Candlish
A fascinating and detailed history of the rivalry between Newcastle United and Sunderland.
Paperback. ISBN 1899807 39 X £14.99

Black Lions - a history of black players in English football
Rodney Hinds
The story of black players in English football, with interviews with players such as Garth Crooks, John Barnes and Luther Blissett. Hardback. Rodney Hinds is the sports editor of The Voice.
Hardback. ISBN 1899807 38 1 £16.99

Rowing with my Wife
Dan Williams
A year in the adventures of a gig rower, the Cornish sport that is spreading around the world.
Paperback. ISBN 1899807 36 5 £7.99

Local Heroes
John Shawcroft
The story of the Derbyshire team which won cricket's county championship in 1936, the only time the county has finished first.
Paperback. ISBN 1899807 35 7 £14.99

Willie Irvine – Together Again
Willie Irvine with Dave Thomas
The remarkable story of the Burnley and Northern Ireland centre forward who grew up in abject poverty, rose to the heights only to fall into depression after he stopped playing. He also found out some remarkable things about his family while researching the book, chiefly that his parents had never married!
Hardback. ISBN 1899807 33 0 £17.99

The Art of Bradman
Difficult to find a new book about the greatest batsman ever. But this is unique. A selection of paintings of the great man from the Bradman Museum at Bowral Oval with text by the museum's curator. A must for every cricket fan's collection.
Leatherbound with gold lettering and red ribbon marker.
ISBN 1899807 32 2 £25

Colin Blythe – lament for a legend
Christopher Scoble
Colin Blythe was a giant in the golden age of county cricket before the First World War. He was the most famous England cricketer to be killed in the conflict. This is the first biography of a complex personality, who was one of the first cricketers to challenge the game's rulers, demanding to handle his own financial affairs.
Hardback. ISBN 1899807 31 4 £16.99

Europe United – a History of the European Cup/ Champions League
Andrew Godsell
The European Cup and its successor, the Champions League, was 50 years old in 2005 and this book celebrates all the great games and characters of the world's greatest club competition.
Hardback. ISBN 1899807 30 6 Price £17.99

Twickenham – the History of the Cathedral of Rugby
Ed Harris
The story of rugby's most famous ground, from its days as a cabbage patch to the multi-million sports arena it is now.
Hardback. ISBN 1899807 29 2 £17.99

Another Bloody Tangle!
Peter Bishop
The author loves fishing, sadly the sport doesn't reciprocate. The Liverpool Echo said: "echoes of the black humour of Alan Bleasdale".
Paperback. ISBN 1899807 28.4 £7.99

The Rebel – Derek Roche – Irish warrior, British champion
Nigel McDermid
The tale of boxing hero Derek Roche is a journey from an Irish council estate to becoming the first Irishman to win a Lonsdale Belt outright. The Guardian said: "refreshingly honest and... genuinely funny".
Paperback. ISBN 1899807 25 X £7.99